FOOTBALL MANAGER STOLE MY LIFE

20 years of beautiful obsession

FOOTBALL MANAGER
STOLE MY LIFE

20 years of beautiful obsession

By Iain Macintosh, Kenny Millar and Neil White

BackPage Press
World-class sports books

Cover photography and design: Freight Design, Glasgow
Designed and typeset by Freight Design, Glasgow

Printed and bound in Poland by OZGraf

www.backpagepress.co.uk

2.5% of the sale of this product will be donated to War Child, charity no.1071659

This goes out to my brother John White,
my co-manager in the glory days – *Neil White*

FOREWORD

Miles Jacobson
Sports Interactive
Summer 2012

Sports Interactive have spent two decades creating and improving a game that has stolen the lives of millions – but it won't stop there.

When Ov and Paul Collyer first started working on a game they called European Champions as teenagers they were football fans who wanted to make a football management game that they wanted to play.

When I first got involved with the studio 17 years ago, it was as a mate helping out a couple of other mates who made a game I'd spent so much of my 'free' time playing.

Who would have thought that 20 years after Ov and Paul's first release, we'd have sold more than 20 million copies of the studio's different games, played for an average of more than 100 hours by each person, every year.

It never ceases to amaze us how many people enjoy our games and the effect it has on them. Just like we were all those years ago, we're still football fans making a game for ourselves that lots of other people seem to enjoy as well. We thank those of you who buy our games every day for allowing us to have made a career out of what is still our hobby!

Over the years, people have got in touch with us, telling us stories about how our games have affected their lives. We've heard comedians using the game as part of their comedy set, as though the games have become part of culture.

We've had musicians telling us how the game keeps them sane (or, in some cases, insane) on tour. Footballers telling us how the game has inspired them to do their coaching badges and get into management when their careers end. We've heard how the game has helped people get through some dark times, as they were able to escape into a parallel world where they were managing a football team.

People talk about their games in the pub as though it's real life. Our amazing research team around the world find great talent before they've made their first team debuts and when people see them play, they know of them from FM.

We even heard people admitting that they only put money on Alan Dzagoev to score the first goal against the Czech Republic in Euro 2012 because they knew of him from FM – with me asking them to donate some of their winnings to War Child, a charity that benefits from every copy of Football Manager sold.

So when BackPage Press approached us asking for some help for a book they were working on to document some of these stories, we were delighted. Especially as they too offered to donate some of the proceeds to War Child!

It's been a great 20 years. But this is only just the beginning of the story of Sports Interactive and our games. All of us at the studio hope to keep making a game that we all want to play for many years to come.

✚ New Manager   ⏱ Game Status   ♥ Customise   ∞ Search

Game name:
CHAMP MAN/FM

Last saved:
AUGUST 10 2012

Game time:
20 YEARS

Addictness rating:
You named your first born Bakayoko. You are Facebook friends with at least one player you once signed. You have been to watch FC To Madeira.

INTRODUCTION

Neil White
BackPage Press, Summer 2012

How one unjust sacking almost destroyed a marriage and inspired a book on the greatest game in the world.

I thought I was alone. We all did.

For years following the split of a turbulent yet triumphant managerial partnership with my younger brother, I had hardly discussed Champ Man with anybody. Those days when I would come back from university and the two of us would sit side-by-side in his room constructing a team around Ariel Ortega were long gone. I was making my way in the world, in a meandering kind of way, but my managerial alter-ego remained a secret identity. My finest hour, when Stirling Albion won the League Cup out of the Third Division and my statue was erected outside Forthbank, was one I did not feel able to share.

Shortly after the epoch-defining front two of Barry Elliott and Scott McLean took Stirling to Hampden, I got a job on the sports desk of The Sunday Times Scotland and realised that I was not alone.

Of the five writers on the desk, only one did not play and that was because he feared that once he loaded the game up, there was every chance he would 'go native'. He was absolutely right, but part of me still regrets never seeing that sprawling database and the spider's web of cause-and-effect decision-making overload this fastidious football mind. I imagine him degenerating into something like Martin Sheen in the final reel of Apocalypse Now, except instead of Marlon Brando, his deranged quest would be for Maxim Tsigalko.

NATHAN SYKES @NathanTheWanted

Bit tired so I am looking forward to this flight so I can get some sleep and keep my league going on #footballmanager with stoke!! :P

The life of an international pop star can't provide the thrill of a late equaliser at Wigan to keep you in the Premier League

The rest of us would talk about the game we were in: me scratching out a reputation in the lower leagues, trying to earn the Falkirk job I cherished, not walk into it; them throwing money around at Rangers, Celtic and Liverpool. Then, one day, the chief football writer, let's call him Douglas Alexander, told me this story.

His pregnant wife returns home from work to find her husband sitting at the breakfast bar in his kitchen, in his suit. His work laptop is open in front of him. His head is in his hands. She asks him what is wrong.

"I can't believe it. They've sacked me."

"What? How? Why? But we're going to have a family! What are we going to do?"

What? Wait... no... it's OK, I mean... it's Liverpool. They've sacked me. I'm second in the league and still in Europe, but we got beat 4-0 off Everton. It's not fair."

Incredibly, Dougie's marriage survived that derby defeat dismissal and baby David is almost old enough to co-manage Liverpool with his old man.

Hearing Dougie's confession, I began to wonder how many more stories were out there. How many lives had been... what's the right word? Touched? Stunted? Destroyed?... by this most immersive of games?

MATTHEW CUNNINGTON @matt_cunnington

@TomBeere @CharlieFayer
Finally we're on #footballmanager
#dreamscometrue

AFC Wimbledon kids make the grade

At every turn in the production of this book, somebody else told us their story: the gamers who sent in their tales, some of which appear in these pages; the Champ Man/FM legends who confessed to signing themselves for Barcelona or Manchester United; the guy on the seat next to BackPage Press on the train to the launch of Graham Hunter's Barcelona book; Andrew and Adrian, at Freight, who designed this book. That pair once spent an Edinburgh-Glasgow train ride discussing strategy for their matches, in character of course. At the end of the line, the lady across from them said: "My son is a footballer, he just got released by Hearts and he's been training with East Fife. What team do you manage?" Andrew and Adrian, faced with the choice of confessing to their delusions or staying with the story, made the right call. "I'm at Aberdeen, he's St Mirren."

 **500**

Lines of code written by Paul and Ov Collyer for European Champions, the game that would become Championship Manager

As we finished putting the book together at the end of the season, I was struck by how every event in football was reflected through the lens of FM. When Harry Redknapp didn't get the England job, Paul Merson commiserated with him, as he hated when that happened to him on Champ Man. When Pep Guardiola left Barcelona, Kevin Bridges sympathised with the burnout suffered by the king of Catalonia, likening the experience to his own CM 01/02 career. When Vincent Kompany led Manchester City to the English title, Twitter was flooded by people reflecting in his glory. After all, it was they who discovered him as a 17-year-old at Anderlecht. And then, when Alan Dzagoev burst out of the blocks with two goals in the first round of matches at Euro 2012, Miles Jacobson was quick to point out that he was both an FM star and an FM player.

Twenty years after it all began, FM is a bigger part of football than ever before. Many of those who live second lives as managers play no other games. They are not gamers, but lovers of football, and FM has become as much a part of that culture for them as watching the game on a Saturday.

This game remains a place where dreams can come true and that should never lose its appeal. You and I can lead our team out in the final of the Champions League (suit and theme music optional). Players who never reach the big leagues can be sold to Real Madrid for £40m (and hear about it from total strangers in late-night takeaway joints) and, thanks to the 20 million copies sold since 1992, FM has helped transform the lives of children in regions devastated by conflict through its incredible partnership with War Child.

Everyone involved in this book enjoyed immensely the process of documenting the cultural phenomenon of Football Manager. We hope it serves well the game we all love.

Thank you very much for buying it and may your dreams continue to come true.

35

Divorce cases in which the game has been cited as a factor in the break-up

23%

The score given to Championship Manager in one early review

SKILL
AND PACE

How to take over the world from your bedroom

This whole thing started in Cheshire, where, in the early 1980s, two young brothers, like many thousands of young people up and down the UK, started to play a game called Football Manager. Written and published by Kevin Toms, an English games designer, this was a game that enabled the early home computers to produce an incredibly immersive management experience. It also gave Paul and Ov Collyer the idea to create their own game, one that soon had their friends hooked, but was rejected by all but two of the 20 publishers they sent it to.

Paul: We had a BBC Micro, because our parents thought it was educational. So we played Football Manager on that.

FMSML: HOW LONG DID IT TAKE YOU GUYS ON YOUR BBC TO GO FROM PLAYING THAT GAME TO TRYING TO WORK OUT HOW YOU COULD DO ONE YOURSELF?

Ov: I don't think we did an actual lot of programming of what became... we messed around on it.

Paul: I did a league table generator, very early, that basically plotted the results for the First Division, as it was then, and it would update the league table. That was my first kind of effort, I think we had a couple of little bits and pieces didn't we?

Ov: What was it, the Amstrad?

Paul: It was the Amstrad when we actually started again, or you started it didn't you, with the skill and pace?

Ov: Skill and pace! For some reason we identified, or I identified, I'll take the blame...

Paul: Well, I think it's pretty fundamental to it, actually.

Ov: I decided that the two main attributes of players were skill and pace. That's it. No passing, heading.

Paul: That's the Arsene Wenger school of thought, skill and pace.

Ov: So yeah, I think it was on the Amstrad, was it the Amstrad 6128, I think? The one with the disc drive, and we messed around with that for ages.

Paul: 1985 I think it started out.

Ov: Maybe a couple of years after that before we got an ST?

BBC

Amstrad

Collyer brothers

I decided that the two main attributes of players were skill and pace. That's it. No passing, no heading.

Paul: We did buy an Atari ST, that's right – proper programming language.

Ov: Then an Amiga 500. Each time we'd rewrite it I think, didn't we, when we went from the ST to the Amiga 500?

Paul: I think we must have rewritten it, because it had to go onto GFA Basic. Then we sort of... I went off to university and spent a few years up there, and we sort of did bits on our own really, then we'd come back at half-term and do nothing but sit across the computer. But you were still at school, so you were probably doing quite a lot from home.

Ov: Yeah it was just kind of on and off really, as a hobby. We just referred to it amongst each other as 'The Game'. You know, 'Have you done any more work on The Game?' Or 'Do you want to go and work on The Game?' It was this kind of constant, it was this nice thing as brothers to have I think.

Paul: I think I left university, dropped out of university because of this, basically. Basically I spent too much time drinking beer and doing The Game, playing The Game. I think that was what, 1990 was it?

Ov: Yeah, about then. I sort of did similar.

Paul: Then we started sending it off, sending letters to people.

Ov: Yeah I think it was the case then that I'd come back from a year at university which I hadn't enjoyed at all, I didn't want to stay there, and we had this sort of thing in the background, we thought, 'Well why don't we see what we can do with it?' All our friends were saying, 'This is really good, this is so much fun to play, why not try something?'

It was a case of just polishing it up a little bit, writing a user guide that I did, photocopied it like 20 times, and sending it off to a bunch of publishers to see what happens.

Atari 1040ST

This is so much fun to play, why not try something?

Amiga 500

EUROPEAN CHAMPIONS

USER GUIDE

BRYAN ROBSON CELEBRATES HIS EQUALIZING GOAL IN THE 1988 EUROPEAN
CHAMPIONSHIP GAME AGAINST EVENTUAL WINNERS HOLLAND.

UPDATED FOR VERSION 1.03

When Paul and Ov Collyer decided to send the game they had developed to publishers, they had to come up with a name. Until then, it had always been 'The Game' played by only the brothers and their friends.

This is the document that accompanied the copies of 'European Champions' that went out to 20 publishers, explaining how the game worked and what made it different from the management simulations on the market.

Most publishers ignored them. Electronic Arts rejected them. However, Domark saw a diamond in the rough and Championship Manager found a home.

SOFTWARE OBJECTIVES SUMMARY

EUROPEAN CHAMPIONS

WHY IS THIS PRODUCT SO UNIQUE?

Football management strategy games are hardly a new idea. Therefore, any new implementation must surely have some fundamental difference which sets it apart. We have identified the reasons our game is unique;

It has great depth. There are 1500 players in the game, each with two screens of information. Although up to four people can play the game, there are also 150 or so computer-controlled managers 'trying' equally hard to succeed. We have written routines in the program that allow the computer-managers to make decisions about team selection, which players to buy and sell to strengthen their squads, whether to make a sub during a match etc. Each club has it's own squad of 16 to 25 players. There are 80 league clubs. People who have played the game have very often spent ages just flicking through the hundreds of player information screens looking at the wealth of information available.

The idea of the computer managers making realistic decisions adds something extra to the game. It becomes even more playable. It adds a vital element of competition to the game. Computer teams' performances are now based on a whole host of factors. Imagine this scenario; The team you are in charge of approaches the last game of the season needing victory to avoid relegation. You select your team, and modify your tactics etc. The computer does likewise. You lead 2-1 with a minute to go. The computer team then scores a last gasp equalizer to condemn you to relegation to division two. Surely it is important that such a crucial moment during gameplay is as a result of a complex input of true-to-life factors (team selection, captains, subs, tactics, playing style etc) rather than the equivalent of a throw of a dice?

/ Here's the secret of Champ Man's success – 150 managers who are trying to beat
you. In 1992, that was a pretty big deal.

USER GUIDE

PLAYER FACTFILES

The player factfiles can be called up virtually everytime a player's name appears on the screen (eg player goalscorers tables, squad lists, transfer list etc). Simply point and click on top of their name.

The factfile screen gives vital information about the player. The following information is displayed;

BASIC INFORMATION

AGE. Obvious.

CLUB. Obvious

PREVIOUS CLUB. Club he was at before current club.

CONTRACT. Gives week of season that contract expires.
The week refers to the week stated at the top of the main menu screen. (eg 12/5 ⇒ contract expires week 12, season 5)

WAGE. Weekly wage.

FUTURE. Unknown → Player is open to approach but not on the transfer list
Staying → Definitely not for sale.
Listed → Was placed on transfer list by his club.
Listed R → Was placed on transfer list at own request.

VALUE. If the player is transfer listed, the value shown is the fee that his club is asking.
If the player is not transfer listed, the value shown is an estimated value- estimated by the coach. (See "player valuations" section).

POS. The positions he can play at (G, D, M, A).

SIDE. The side he plays at (R, L, Centre)

/ The basic DNA of the transfer system is here. No agents to muddy the waters.

─ 20 ─

USER GUIDE

PASSING. Accuracy of passing.

TACKLING. Accuracy of tackling.

PACE. How fast he is.

HEADING. Ability to head the ball.

FLAIR. The potential to do the unexpected

CREATIVITY. The skill of creating goalscoring chances

} Relative strengths and weaknesses.
eg. how Passing compares with Tackling et.

AGGRESSION. A hard man or a wimp?

INFLUENCE. How well he influences/help his team mates

AVAILABILITY. Whether injured (& type of injury et), or suspended.
Also indicates match fitness, and whether picked (& shirt no.)

APPS. No. of appearances.

GOALS. Goals scored.

DISP. Disciplinary points gained (Booking 5pts, Sending Off 20 pts)

AV R. Average match rating.

MIN R. Minimum match rating

MAX R. Maximum match rating

This information is available for the current season being played, and the last season.

MORALE. Long term morale.

FUTURE PLANS. The player's loyalty to the club. Does he want to leave?

At the top right of the screen are a number of other options;

STA. Used to adjust a player's transfer status (i.e. whether listed etc)

BUY Used to approach a player.

ADD used to add a player to a shortlist.

/ Already, the search for a dependable 7/10 full-back had begun

- II -

USER GUIDE

STRATEGIES

The manager must select a formation and style of football to suit the squad he has.

His formation must be a compromise; it must provide enough attacking play, without leaving his defence too vulnerable. He must be able to adjust it to suit different opponents.

His team should be balanced; there should be players both on the right and the left. He must be able to modify his tactics to deal with different circumstances (eg 2-0 down with 20 minutes to go).

The manager can choose from the following contrasting styles of play;

CONTINENTAL STYLE. Slow build up with sudden lightning fast attacking moves. Requires players with technical ability.

CLOSE PASSING STYLE Fast, intelligent passes to feet. Defence rapidly transformed into attack.

DIRECT STYLE Balls played directly to players in attacking positions, eg instant through balls etc.

LONG BALL STYLE Long high balls played to forward players. High accurate balls.

UP-AND-UNDER STYLE. Ball booted upfield towards goal for forwards to chase. A less attractive style of play. Opposition kept under pressure from aerial bombardment.

When he selects his team, the players selected must be suitable for the role they are to play in the team. The manager must consider the skills required for a certain playing position within the framework of a certain style of play. His captain must have qualities usually associated with being a captain.

/ No false No.9s here, thank you very much

ANT & DEC

Ant & Dec received a unique leaving gift on their last day hosting Saturday morning show SMTV Live in 2001. The pair – self-confessed Newcastle supporters and Champ Man addicts – received a letter from Sports Interactive along with special edition copies of Championship Manager 2001/02. Ant featured in the Newcastle squad, valued at £4.7 million with a weekly wage of £50,000. Dec, on the other hand, was dumped at Sunderland, with a mere £90 for a virtual pay packet.

ANT & DEC were among the fortunate few to receive personalised copies of the game. Both are passionate Newcastle United fans, so it's credit to the bond between these kings of light entertainment that their partnership survived the machiavellian move of placing Declan Donnelly at Sunderland.

We've got a rejection letter from Electronic Arts, haven't we?

Paul: We've got a letter haven't we from Electronic Arts?

Miles: Yeah we've got a rejection letter from Electronic Arts with the tea stain where Ov left his tea.

Paul: Do you know where that is by the way?

Miles: Yeah, I know where we've got scans of it all, anyway. Duffy's got them hidden. And the original user guide somewhere as well.

Ov: I think I sent it to around 20 publishers, and only two or three replied I think. EA were saying, 'There's no graphics, it's got to compete with these games, it's not going to work, why don't you advertise it in the back of a magazine?' I mean, it's fair enough, that was what their opinion was.

Miles: At least they gave us advice.

Paul: Yeah they did.

Ov: Exactly. They didn't just ignore it like most of them. I think then we'd had Domark interested, which of course became Eidos later on.

Paul: Thalamus.

Ov: And Thalamus. It was sort of a toss-up between the two, Thalamus seemed to be just run by one guy, a really nice bloke, he really helped us and made us a very fair offer, and Domark was the other one. We kind of, a little bit sneakily, played them off against each other in our naive way, thinking we were really clever.

Paul: We ended up with a rubbish deal.

Ov: Yeah, a crap deal.

Miles: That was also before I was here.

There's no graphics, it's got to compete with these games, it's not going to work, why don't you advertise it in the back of a magazine?

Paul: We presented it to them as a game called European Champions. Have you got the documents on that?

Ov: It is somewhere, I think with the user guide yeah, a picture of Bryan Robson on the front in an England shirt celebrating. When was it, when they played Holland, it wasn't in Holland.

Paul: '88.

Ov: The European Championships. Yeah '88.

Paul: So that's probably five years. Five years of varying degrees of intensity, kind of as and when. I think it's fair to say that Oliver put a lot of time into his document and sending it around. I think you got the idea that this was something we could do with, because we just played it with our mates on Saturdays didn't we? Just around the TV.

FMSML: SO YOU GO WITH DOMARK, HAVE YOU LEFT HOME AT THIS STAGE OR ARE YOU STILL LIVING WITH YOUR FOLKS?

Ov: You would have left home.

Paul: I'd left home.

Ov: I would have just come back from my year at Leeds Uni, so I would have been back at home.

Paul: I'd been living in Liverpool, because I'd given up university by then.

Ov: Yeah, when we went to meet Domark for the first time in London, you weren't at home because we met at the station, Paddington or Euston or something. It was really exciting.

Paul: I remember one time we went to see Domark in London and we drove back to Liverpool so fast in your little car, was it a Fiesta you had?

Ov: Yeah.

Paul: It felt like about an hour and a half or something like that, I'll never forget that journey. He was a psycho driver when he was younger.

Ov: Yeah. Not good.

Paul: Don't do it kids. Do you remember when we went to see Domark, and they sort of told us what they thought and then said, 'Yeah, well, it's a good idea – we're just going to bolt some graphics onto it'.

Ov: 'Bolt some graphics onto it'. That's right, yeah.

FMSML: DID YOU HAVE TO BE QUITE PROTECTIVE OF WHAT YOU GUYS WANTED TO DO TO IT?

Ov: We were very protective weren't we?

Paul: Not in the right way, but yeah.

Ov: In terms of the game, not in terms of the important stuff. It didn't even cross our mind, the name, the IP [intellectual property], the ownership or anything like that, would you agree with that Paul?

Paul: Oh yeah, no it didn't cross our mind. We didn't have any idea whatsoever.

Ov: We didn't even know what IP was. They're publishing it, we're writing it, and they're going to give us some money. What can go wrong?

Whizz kid students, left, Oliver and Paul Collyer.

Paul: I mean if we'd have had Miles's business sense when we were like 19 years old or whatever then fine, we might've done it quicker or better. But I don't think that's realistic is it, because you can't be everything, and the people that make these games aren't the type of people that can have this sort of foresight.

Miles: We wouldn't have been able to do any of this without that initial deal. So whilst we don't talk about it ending, we have to still give props to the guys at Domark for giving the game a chance in the first place, and without the guys at Domark I wouldn't have got involved either.

Brothers' play pays off

Two enterprising Shropshire brothers have proved that play can pay.

Paul and Oliver Collyer from Church Stretton have sold a football computer game after developing it in their spare time.

The former Church Stretton School students found three firms bidding against each other for the publishing rights to the game.

They now stand to get substantial royalties in addition to the sale fee and there is an option for a follow up.

"There is even the possibility of it being translated into French and German," said proud mum, Judy Collyer.

"To think I used to moan about the time they spent crouched over a screen," she said.

Paul (23) and Oliver (19) developed the game over three to four years. Oliver took a year off before going to university to add the finishing touches.

THE WORLD ACCORDING TO FM

One man's journey inside
the alternative reality of
Champ Man 01/02

Iain Macintosh's instructions were simple: obtain a copy of
Championship Manager 01/02. Start her up. Go on holiday. Observe.
Report back. This is one man's account of how things could have
been if only real life was more like Champ Man

Ah, there you are! Welcome to the Football Manager time machine! We're pretty sketchy on the science, but we think that with a couple of AA batteries and those jump leads behind you, there's just a chance we can take you back to a far simpler time. A time when the only games that Lionel Messi was dominating were the ones at his 14th birthday party. A time when the only oil money at Manchester City was in the catering budget and a time when Roman Abramovich had much better things to do with his cash. This is the time of Championship Manager 2001/02. Manchester United have just won their third consecutive title, but Sir Alex Ferguson plans to retire at the end of the season.

In Italy, Roma rule the roost, In Spain, it's Real Madrid who prosper while Barcelona are a shadow of their former selves. The Catalans only just qualified for the Champions League last season! Can they recover? Come on, step inside the pod, quickly now, cover your eyes. It gets a little bumpy. Oh, and don't worry if some poo comes out, that's perfectly normal...

FAZAM!

2002

All hail Portugal and their golden generation! With goals from Luis Figo, Joao Pinto and Rui Costa, they topple Italy in the World Cup Final in Tokyo and set down the foundations for a new era of supremacy. England, by brutal contrast, are knocked out in the second round. By Germany. On penalties. Again.

In the Premier League, Sir Alex Ferguson signs off with a bang, beating Roma to win the Champions League and sealing Manchester United's record fourth successive title. Pausing only to shout at a passing cloud and ban a nearby journalist from the county of Lancashire, he retires to spend more time with his horses and is replaced by Leeds boss David O'Leary. Fergie's United finish 10 points ahead of Arsenal, largely due to new signing Ruud van Nistelrooy's astonishing record of 42 goals in 54 games. Arsenal, whose season is derailed by the defection of Patrick Vieira to Barcelona in a £38m deal, console themselves with the FA Cup. To the surprise of absolutely no-one, Arsene Wenger opts to keep the Vieira windfall, claiming, "it's for a rainy day." Elsewhere, a young forward by the name of Tonton Zola Moukoko breaks into the Derby side, scoring seven goals in 12 games, Kenny Dalglish saves Charlton from the drop and Southampton are relegated.

If Vieira left in search of a league title, he was disappointed. Despite Patrick Kluivert's 32-goal season, Real Madrid, who snaffle Francesco Totti in a £37m deal in January, squeak home by a single point. In Italy, vanquished Champions League losers Roma do at least pip AC Milan to the Serie A title, thanks to 66 goals from Gabriel Batistuta and Vincenzo Montella. Meanwhile in Scotland, Celtic finish first and Rangers finish second.

2003

It is not a good day to be David O'Leary. But then it never is, is it? Having left Leeds for Manchester United, the Irishman can only watch in horror as Manchester United are comfortably beaten into second place by...erm...Leeds. His replacement Roy Hodgson, having prospered on the continent, finally proves himself in his home country, guiding the Yorkshire side to their first league title in 11 years. Chairman Peter Ridsdale tells journalists that he feels like he is, "living the dream," and does his best to ignore the threatening-looking envelopes on the doorstep. Liverpool trot home in third and Fulham, now managed by Graham Rix since Jean Tigana took the France job, pick up the final Champions League place at the expense of Arsenal. Gunners fans, however, are too busy laughing at the relegation of Tottenham Hotspur to care. Shamed Spurs boss Glenn Hoddle angrily blames his players for sins committed in this and any other past lives and refuses to explain why he thought re-signing Ruel Fox was a good idea. Down in south-east London, a chap by the name of Cherno Samba is scoring goals at the rate of 1.1 a game for Millwall and elsewhere Southampton are relegated again, this time to the third flight.

Roma are the undisputed power on the continent. Fabio Capello's side, having lured in Luis Figo in the summer, leave their rivals in the dust in Serie A and wallop Barcelona 4-1 in the Champions League final. At the start of the season Barca spend £40m on Juventus pair Lilian Thuram and Gianluigi Buffon, but Real Madrid snap up Rui Costa and beat the Catalans to the title again. Patrick Vieira kicks the club cat. Meanwhile in Scotland, Celtic finish first and Rangers finish second.

2004

Revenge! In a replay of the 2002 World Cup Final, Italy turn the tables on Portugal in the European Championships and beat them 2-1 in Lisbon. It is a feat all the more spectacular when you learn that Italian manager Giovanni Trapattoni retired two days before the final and left his players to their own devices. Now that's hands-off management. England, by brutal contrast, lose all three group games and Sven-Goran Eriksson is sacked.

Still, it's finally a good day to be David O'Leary! Never afraid to splash the cash, the Manchester United boss shells out for Jaap Stam, Zinedine Zidane and...er...Gary O'Neil. His spending spree pays off and he almost leads his team to an unprecedented domestic treble, winning the league and the FA Cup, but losing the League Cup to Louis van Gaal's Newcastle. Liverpool finish second, despite the signings of Martin Keown, Gianluca Festa and Chris Perry, while Leeds and Arsenal finish third and fourth. Tottenham return to the Premier League at the first time of asking, led by bearded Australian David Mitchell whose madcap attacking 4-2-1-2-1 formation baffles the second flight into submission. Ruel Fox is crammed into a cardboard box and shipped to Miami. Cherno Samba is signed by Newcastle for £10m, while Ipswich lay out £5m for Tonton Zola Moukoko. Kenny Dalglish is sacked by Charlton, but pops up again at Aston Villa, while Southampton lose the play-off final and consign themselves to the third flight for a second season.

Still, Patrick Vieira's happy. Barcelona clean up, winning the Champions League, La Liga, the Spanish Cup and a prestigious Scrabble tournament in Minorca where Frank de Boer drops 'quizzical' over a triple word score. Javier Saviola and Patrick Kluivert hit 73 goals between them as Real Madrid are beaten into third place behind Valencia. In Italy, Roma nonchalantly pick up their fourth consecutive Serie A title with an asset-stripped Juventus slumping into 12th. Meanwhile in Scotland, Celtic finish first and Rangers finish second.

2005

Roma are back on top in Europe, snatching the Champions League from Barcelona's tiny mitts and lifting it above their heads for the second time in three years. Fabio Capello's side are making life very dull indeed in Italy. There they seal their fifth consecutive title having reversed the talent drain to Spain by buying Roberto Carlos and former Middlesbrough soul-glo poster boy Emerson, as well as Juan Sebastian Veron who takes his leave of Old Trafford after four glorious years.

Veron's departure does little to stem the flow of trophies. David O'Leary picks up his second title in a row and credits his success to, "all the children everywhere," because, as he sagely adds, "the children are our future." Man Utd beat off a determined challenge from Louis van Gaal's Newcastle whose 4-5-1 is spearheaded by Cherno Samba to devastating effect. The former Millwall man scores 21 goals and makes his debut for new England manager...er...Dave Jones, scoring twice. Arsenal and Leeds make up the other Champions League places, Kenny Dalglish's Aston Villa are relegated and poor old Southampton plummet into the fourth division. Tottenham, in a act of gross spitefulness, sack Mitchell after finishing 16th in their first season back in the Premier League. They replace him with Dalglish.

In Spain, Barcelona win La Liga again, despite not signing anyone for two years. Real Madrid, who have exercised no such discretion in the transfer market having signed Alessandro Del Piero for £28m, are runners-up. Meanwhile in Scotland, Celtic finish first and Rangers finish second.

 MARK KERR

A fringe player at Leeds United, Mark moved from Falkirk to Hibernian in 2001, then to Sunderland in 2002 and finally to Elland Road in 2003. A determined and cultured midfielder, Kerr has over 50 caps for Scotland and is valued at £3.5m

 WORLD PLAYER OF THE YEAR

2002 — Gabriel Batistuta (Roma)

2003 — Vincenzo Montella (Roma)

2004 — Javier Saviola (Barcelona)

2005 — Hernan Crespo (Lazio)

2006 — Amoroso (Dortmund)

2007 — Vincenzo Montella (Roma)

2008 — Juan Sebastian Veron (Roma)

2009 — Javier Saviola (Barcelona)

2010 — Pablo Aimar (Arsenal)

2011 — To Madeira (Dortmund)

 MIKE DUFF

A consistently excellent right-back, it's a wonder that 33-year-old Duff didn't achieve more. Now with QPR in the second flight, he has also played for Cheltenham, Darlington, Wolves and Brighton, never averaging less than 7.50 in a season.

2006

The world dances to the sound of the samba beat as Brazil lift their fifth World Cup, this time in Berlin. Felipao, in his second spell as manager, utilises a very dull 4-4-2 with Ronaldo and Amoroso up front, and grinds his way to victory over Holland. England, by brutal contrast, are knocked out in the second round. By Brazil. On penalties. Again. Frankly, it's hard to comprehend how a team manned by the likes of Chris Kirkland, Sam Sodje and former Crewe midfielder David Wright can fall so short on the big stage.

It's three titles in a row for David O'Leary at Old Trafford. Christian Vieri and Ruud van Nistelrooy score freely to hold off the challenge of Dalglish's renewed and revitalised Tottenham. Spurs now boast the attacking talents of Carl Cort to support the deadly finishing of Steffen Iversen. What? What's so funny? Arsenal finish third, Liverpool come fourth and Walter Smith's Everton, who have just moved into a 55,000 all-seater, retractable-roofed stadium on King's Docks, are relegated. Southampton, after a shaming season in the fourth division, are promoted into the third.

The Roman Empire has fallen... and has been replaced by a different Roman Empire. Lazio, who snaffle Zidane on a Bosman after his two seasons with Man Utd, end Roma's run of five consecutive titles, romping home eight points clear. Across Italy, there are street parties and carnivals, mopeds are tossed about in the air like children's toys. Poor Roma even lose the Champions League final to Bayern Munich. Capello pushes a policeman over. In Spain, after 18 months of frugality, Barcelona finally spend some money, bringing in David Beckham for £14m, Albert Nadj for £5m and Mark Iuliano for £9m. They finish second to Real Madrid, who didn't spend a penny. There is no logic. Meanwhile in Scotland, Celtic finish first and Rangers finish second.

2007

After 17 years of hurt, Liverpool are the English champions once again. Across Merseyside and the home counties, there are street-parties and carnivals, curly-haired, moustachioed men and women dance the night away and nine months from now there will be a boom of curly haired, moustachioed babies. It's taken nine years of tinkering, but Gerard Houllier finally delivers and then goes on to win the FA Cup for good measure. Arsenal finish second, Newcastle, with Cherno Samba hitting 31 goals, finish third and Chelsea troop home in fourth under Rudi Voller. The German boss is building quite a side, snatching Tonton Zola Moukoko from Ipswich and adding him to an illustrious line-up that includes Marco Di Vaio, Roy Makaay and Michael Duberry.

David O'Leary's Man Utd, despite blowing £43m on Diego Tristan, Damiano Zenoni and Jens Nowotny tumble to eighth. Perhaps their downfall was caused by Roy Keane's departure to Atalanta. Perhaps it was the loss of Jaap Stam to Dortmund. Or perhaps, just perhaps, it was the rash decision to sell indefatigable Wes Brown to Roma for £23m.

Not that Brown's recruitment helps Fabio Capello one iota, of course. Nor does his cunning plan to steal Pavel Nedved from Lazio. Roma slip to third while their rivals retain the title. Fabio Capello pushes a police horse over. Lazio, still powered by Zinedine Zidane and made potent by Andrey Shevchenko, snatch the title by a point from Juventus. They also win the Champions League, beating Bayern 2-1. In Spain, Barcelona spend big again, whacking £28m on Wilfried Bouma and another £11m on Sol Campbell. It works and the title is theirs. Patrick Kluivert, by the way, has now scored 221 goals in six seasons. Meanwhile in Scotland, Celtic finish first and Rangers finish second.

2008

Arrigo Sacchi's Italy retain the European Championships in Stockholm with a crushing 3-0 defeat of dark horses Romania. Luca Toni scores a hat-trick. England finally survive a summer tournament without getting knocked out on penalties. Instead, Dave Jones' men are knocked out in normal time at the quarter-final stage by Ukraine.

Ken Bates has ruled Chelsea since 1982 and finally, finally, finally, his team have won the title. A clearly emotional Bates reflects upon a phonecall he took from an unnamed Russian businessman in 2003, saying, "Do you know, I almost sold the club to that c**t. What was I thinking? He probably didn't have any money anyway..."

Arsenal finish second again prompting a furious rant from Arsene Wenger who blames the referees, the Highbury pitch and the excess fluoride in the water. As quickly as it began, however, Liverpool's reign is over. Gerard Houllier's side win the League Cup, but finish outside the Champions League places in fifth. Joe Kinnear's Blackburn come third while David O'Leary, clinging on to the United job by his fingernails, claims fourth. Southampton are relegated back to the basement with a whimper.

Roma's golden age is over as well. Even the acquisition of Italian hero Luca Toni can't lift them from third and Lazio win the title again. You have to go back to 1999 to find the last time a team outside Rome won Serie A. Juventus, who hired Marco Tardelli after that awful 12th place finish in 2004, come second. In La Liga, Vicente Del Bosque's static 4-4-2 isn't working. Real Madrid slide into third, overtaken by Carlos Bianchi's Valencia who use a 4-1-2-1-2 with John Carew and Salva up top to break up the duopoly. Barcelona, of course, win the title, their second in a row. Manager Charly Rexach has now won four leagues and nine cups. Meanwhile in Scotland, Celtic finish first and Rangers finish second

① ENGLISH PLAYER OF THE YEAR

2002 — **Ruud van Nistelrooy**
(Man Utd)

2003 — **Ruud van Nistelrooy**
(Man Utd)

2004 — **Mark Viduka**
(Leeds)

2005 — **Ruud van Nistelrooy**
(Man Utd)

2006 — **Cherno Samba**
(Newcastle)

2007 — **Marco di Vaio**
(Chelsea)

2008 — **Thierry Henry**
(Arsenal)

2009 — **Cherno Samba**
(Newcastle)

2010 — **Ronaldinho**
(Liverpool)

2011 — **Michael Duberry**
(Nottingham Forest)

TO MADEIRA

A slow burner, this unheard-of Portuguese striker first came to prominence at Benfica where he scored almost a goal a game for eight years. That finally brought him his big money move to Dortmund and the 2011 World Player of the Year Award. Where did this goal machine spring from?

2009

Money may not buy you happiness, but it does make success in football a little easier. After burning through an eye-watering £74m and buying global luminaries Wes Brown, Harry Kewell, Igor Biscan and David Trezeguet, Inter Milan win the Champions League, beating Juventus 3-2. Sadly for new manager Giuseppe Pillon, Inter miss out on Serie A, losing a two-legged play-off to Lazio, who claim their fourth consecutive title under Alberto Zaccheroni.

It's all change in England where Liverpool snatch back the title, with David Moyes' West Ham, who have somehow retained Joe Cole and Jermain Defoe, trailing just behind. Arsenal and Leeds make up the European places while champions Chelsea finish seventh and manager Rudi Voller is sacked. Manchester United drop to 14th, only seven points above the relegation zone, and lose the League Cup Final to a Clint Hill-inspired Watford. Chairman Martin Edwards, when questioned on David O'Leary's future, mumbles something about him having photographs of, "that awkward episode in the bathroom" and offers the Irishman an extended contract. Grimsby are promoted to the Premier League, as are Wrexham, who sneak through via the play-offs. Southampton reach the fourth division play-off final, but lose to Shrewsbury. Owner Rupert Lowe dryly suggests changing the name of the stadium from St Mary's to St Jude's, but no-one gets the 'patron saint of lost causes' joke and his car is set alight.

These are dark days for Real Madrid, they slip all the way to sixth, while Barcelona, for whom Saviola (185) and Kluivert (275) have now scored 460 goals in eight seasons, lift the title again. Meanwhile in Scotland, Celtic finish fir- what? Good heavens! In Scotland, Rangers finish first and Celtic finish second! The world has been turned upside down!

◎◎ MICHAEL DUNWELL

A prodigious goalscorer for Bishop Auckland, Dunwell was given his big break by Exeter and he didn't disappoint. He scored 81 goals in five seasons before being snapped up by Sheffield Wednesday in 2008. He is worth £6m.

◎◎ JUSTIN GEORCELIN

Having started his career at Northampton, Georcelin could never have imagined that he'd end up at Manchester United. A move to Hull, and 62 goals in three seasons, put him on their radar and he didn't disappoint. Now worth £9m, he's scored 47 goals in 60 games.

After burning through £74m on global luminaries Wes Brown, Harry Kewell, Igor Biscan and David Trezeguet, Inter win the Champions League

2010

Towering Sevilla forward Xisco is the King of the World. It's his goal that seals Spain's first ever World Cup win after a nervous final against Paul Le Guen's France. Dave Jones' England, of course, are knocked out in the quarter-finals, which is, in fairness the best that anyone has done since Sir Bobby Robson in 1990.

For the first time since 1927, Newcastle win the league. Manager Louis van Gaal spends two days celebrating and then hotfoots it to Deportivo. There's no prizes for guessing the player of the year. With an astonishing 50 goals in 65 games for the Magpies, 24-year-old Cherno Samba ensures that he will never have to buy a drink on Tyneside again. Liverpool, who swipe Ronaldinho from Paris St Germain, finish second, with Arsenal and Leeds in third and fourth. Chelsea manager Tommy Svensson is sacked after just six months and replaced by, yes, you've guessed it, Kenny Dalglish. They finish sixth with David O'Leary's broken Man Utd in eighth. Grimsby finish ninth under Peter Taylor, but Wrexham are sent packing, ending the season with just 16 points. Manchester City fall into the third division where they'll meet Southampton, who win the fourth.

In Europe, Dortmund doom Juventus to a second consecutive set of runners-up medals in the Champions League, but consolation comes with the capture of the Serie A title, finally bringing an end to ten years of Roman supremacy. Lazio drop to third, Roma slide to fifth and Fabio Capello pushes a police van down a flight of steps in the city centre and runs away, claiming that, "a group of bigger boys did it." He is later sacked.

In Spain, Real Madrid are in real trouble. For the first time in living memory, they lose more games than they win and finish in eighth. Somehow Vicente del Bosque keeps his job. Over at Barca, Charly Rexach has a job for life after dropping just 11 points all season, finishing first 35 points ahead of Valencia. Meanwhile in Scotland, Celtic finish first and Rangers finish second. Phew.

> For the first time since 1927, Newcastle win the league. Louis van Gaal spends two days celebrating then hot foots it to Deportivo

 STEFAN SELAKOVIC

A star for Halmstad, Selakovic was brought to England by Leicester, but it was Middlesbrough where he spent the bulk of his career. Sadly, the Swede could never recreate his Filbert Street form and was released on a free in 2009.

2011

Porto are the surprise winners in Europe, overturning a subdued Barcelona side still mourning the departure of Patrick Kluivert, who retired in the summer. The Dutchman isn't the only one to call it a day. In England, Gerard Houllier steps down, hands the reins to coach David Preece and the former Luton maestro seals the title in his first season. It's Liverpool's third Premier League in five years. Emile Mpenza leads the way in the scoring stakes, while Pablo Aimar pulls the strings for the resurgent Reds. Not that they can recreate their European glory days. No English team has reached the Final of the Champions League since Sir Alex Ferguson's last Man Utd side. Kenny Dalglish's Chelsea come second, three goals ahead of Rudi Voller's Newcastle. David O'Leary finally runs out of credit with the Man Utd board as Martin Edwards feels that no revelations could be as bad as another season above the relegation zone. With United in thirteenth, he pulls the trigger and replaces the Irishman with Gareth Southgate, who has done such a good job with Arbroath.

 MAXIM TSIGALKO

A lightning quick hitman, Tsigalko moved from Dinamo Minsk to Hamburg in 2003 and scored consistently for club and country. Valued at £6m, he and strike partner Louis Saha are a formidable force.

 RYAN WILLIAMS

A classic tale of rags to riches, Williams moved from Hull to Nottingham Forest to Portsmouth, scoring and making goals all the way before catching the eye of Tottenham, where he won the title. Now 32, he's worth £2.4m.

JUSTIN TOMLINSON MP @JTomlinsonMP

Capello's quit... If they miss my skills on #footballmanager I'd go for Martin O'Neill, but I guess public will want Redknapp.

KB knows burn-out is no laughing matter

 KEVIN BRIDGES @kevinbridges86

Know how Pep feels, been there myself in Champ Man 01/02. Give it a month, your bosmans arrive, arranging friendlies...The love comes back.

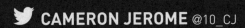 **CAMERON JEROME** @10_CJ

Managing Barca on Football Manager. Just signed myself for £6.5m. The fans are disappointed. They haven't even given me a chance.

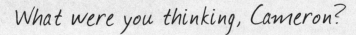

What were you thinking, Cameron?

MILES JACOBSON @milessi

So earlier in the week, Football Manager was mentioned in Emmerdale. And this morning, it was mentioned on Desert Island Discs. #surreal

In Italy, new Roma boss Francesco Guidolin comes within a play-off of retrieving the title, losing to Juventus thanks to a Kieron Dyer brace. In Spain, Sevilla become the first non Barca/Real club to top La Liga since Deportivo in 2000. World Cup winner Xisco leads the way. Barca slip to second, while Real Madrid finish eighth again, their third successive season outside of the top six. Meanwhile in Scotland, Celtic finish first and Rangers, oh you know this by now... Oh yes, and someone called To Maderia wins the World Player of the Year award after scoring 48 in 48 for Dortmund. Strange, I've never actually heard of the man... Extraordinary, isn't it? A hideous dystopian version of our present, warped and contorted out of recognition. Manchester City are a third division club, Manchester United are a spent force, Lionel Messi is an unknown chimney sweep in Buenos Aires and Cristiano Ronaldo is serving tables in a bar in Lisbon. Well, let's go home, eh?

What's that? Really? You want to stay? Well... there's no accounting for taste. Let's have those jump-leads back. Now, step out of the pod, would you? Thank you. I'll just lock up...there, we're all set.

Oh, I forgot to mention, in this reality Tony Blair didn't step down, the Spice Girls never broke up and that Keith Chegwin 'naked' gameshow is now the nation's favourite programme! Seeya!

Iain Macintosh was exploring the world according to Championship Manager 01/02. If you want to spend more time there, why not visit **www.champman0102.co.uk.** You can download the game, including updates that enable you to play today's teams, old school-style, or just spend hours talking about Ryan Williams. It's your call.

 JOAO PAIVA

A bit part player at El Nacional, Paiva made just 24 appearances, scoring 14 goals and spending a large chunk of his adult life on the bench.

FAZAM!

SHALL WE SING A SONG FOR YOU?

How 1990s indie music provided
the backbeat for Champ Man

Somebody wrote, in the early 1990s, that comedy was the new rock 'n' roll.
But comedy had been around for longer than the old rock 'n' roll. In the same
decade, one of gaming's greatest franchises, Grand Theft Auto, was created
by a company that would end the 90s calling itself Rockstar. Meanwhile,
the equivalent of a garage band on an independent label was setting sales
records every year with a football management simulation.

Sports Interactive had one foot in rock 'n' roll from
the start. This is a story that features Blur, one
of the most famous bands of the past 20 years;
Jesus Jones, international bright young things in
the early 1990s, and Elevate, a band with a bass
player who knew one or two things about the
Italian lower leagues.

It's also about an A&R man at Food, the label
behind all but one of those bands, who ended up
running the studio that, all these years later, is still
kicking out the jams.

Miles: I had friends at Domark [the publishers of
Championship Manager] and I had been mucking
about with some data updates anyway, for the
game. I had been talking to Domark about doing
a Jesus Jones game – I was working in the
music industry and Jesus Jones at the time were
massive. The Domark guys wanted to see Blur
play and I gave them a couple of tickets. In return,
they put me in touch with, it was you, originally, Ov.

Ov: Yeah, I remember getting sent ideas for the
game from this Miles character.

Miles: They put us in touch because they knew
I was a fan of the game. I helped out with some
testing and some data. Somehow I've ended up
running the studio, 17 years later.

/ Jesus Jones, transatlantic guitar pop peddlers who almost had their very own computer game

FMSML: DO YOU EVER FEEL LIKE REVIVING THE JESUS JONES GAME?

Miles: No. But I had a big birthday and they played at the party and they were absolutely awesome.

Paul: They must be playing loads.

Miles: No, they hadn't done a gig for well over a year. They were really good. No plans for a new Jesus Jones game, but I am still in touch with them, and a lot of people from that time in music.

FMSML: SO IT WAS RESEARCH TO BEGIN WITH THEN IT SEEMS LIKE YOU JUST...

Miles: Well... I don't really know.

Ov: It is sort of a blurry time.

Miles: I was doing research. I was doing QA [quality assurance], and then I started doing some research and then I got asked to do the whole of the UK research while I was also doing the data updates and had a full-time job as A&R guy.

I didn't want anything for it, I kept coming into the studio and Ov was like, 'We have to pay you something'. Well, no you don't. I was just happy to be part of it, it was just fun.

And then I got to know Paul. He was in a band called Elevate, who I really liked. It was interesting. Every time they had a commercial song and someone would think 'That's great, that could be a hit!' they'd immediately rewrite it so that it was more difficult.

/ The two albums released by Elevate and, below, the band in action, with Paul Collyer on bass (right)

Paul: That's alright, I'm quite proud of that.

Miles: I didn't end up signing them [to Food] because of that. Actually, you chose to sign somewhere else.

Paul: Yeah, well, that wasn't my decision.

Miles: It doesn't matter if it was, I'm glad. Let's be honest.

Paul: You'd have made us work.

Miles: Yeah, probably.

Paul: Probably wouldn't have done this [Football Manager].

FMSML: DID YOU GUYS KNOW EACH OTHER BEFORE THEN? WERE YOU GUYS ALREADY WORKING...

Miles: I knew Ov through the game. I didn't really know Paul, and Ov had said his brother was playing in a band. Paul wasn't in the studio much, so when I was popping into the studio I'd see Ov.

Paul: I was basically working at 40% wasn't I? I was working 40% on the game and 60% doing the music, for about two years or something.

/ *A youthful and angelic Blur, around about the time Miles Jacobson worked with them at Food records*

Miles: And because I'd only pop in during the evenings, that would be when Paul would be playing or rehearsing, so we hadn't got to know each other that well. I went to see the band, really liked them and that's when we got started talking on that score and that's when Ov told me about some contractual issues as well, and asked if I could help out, because I was used to being on the other side of the table.

Ov: Then you took a look at our contracts and...

Miles: ... cried. So I started doing that, I was just doing it to help my mates out. I then got more and more involved, just very organically over the years, until a point when Paul was in Sweden. I started doing all the dealing with the publisher. The chairman of the publisher had sent Ov a fax and you'd written 'f*** off' in a big black marker pen on the fax and faxed it back.

That was the time I started helping out.

Ov: So we decided to go for a more diplomatic negotiating style.

Miles: Which is amazing because I'm not a diplomat, but I was still more diplomatic than Ov.

Ov: I was very relieved when you took that away.

Miles: And apart from putting the odd idea in I wasn't that involved creatively, and then Paul was living in Sweden for a few years, and Ov actually... you decided to leave didn't you?

Ov: I decided to leave, I wasn't even going to come back.

Paul: I was working away from the office for a few years, working from Sweden just from home, and Oliver's walking round the jungle in Vietnam or something like that.

Miles: I had a phone call going, 'Do you want to be MD?'

Ov: Can you take care of this please?

Miles: 'I've still got all these other jobs that I'm doing'. I tried to carry the other jobs on for about four months and realised that wasn't really going to work so I moved my other companies to SI's office and did that for about another year until I realised that I couldn't actually do the other things as well, and just went full-time. That was in about 2001 and then we went through the whole CM4 thing, and that was the point we all realised we had to professionalise the studio, rather than it being just a bunch of kids making games.

FMSML: WAS THAT THE POINT YOU FOCUSED MORE ON THE GAME THAN THE MUSIC OR WERE YOU STILL 60/40 IN FAVOUR OF THE BAND?

Paul: Well we're talking 1994, 1995 or something. I think it was about 95-96 we just stopped doing the music, or I stopped doing the music. I had to decide and it was becoming clear that, well, we'd been relatively successful with the game, but it was becoming clear that we had to put everything into it, it needed my full attention. And I think I enjoyed it more as well.

Miles: It's better than being a fat bass player isn't it?

Paul: I wasn't fat then.

Miles: Did that come afterwards?

Paul: Well it came when I stopped jumping around on stage, I was always short so, and coming here and having 10 beers every night...

Miles: Yes, that's true.

Paul: So yeah, about '96 or something like that and I think that's around the time when we moved to our first sort of bigger office on Upper Street, 96/97.

Miles: It was '95 we moved there, I think, 95/96.

Paul: Yeah so it coincides with that first stage of professionalising if you like.

Miles: Yeah.

Paul: Like, 'This is what we do now'. No more messing around.

THE FM PLAYLIST
It's not just the games charts that FM dominates. Several of the best-selling and most-respected artists on planet pop are FM players. Here we reveal the inspiration behind some of their biggest hits.

1 Let Me Entertain You (with my attacking wing-backs)
Robbie Williams

2 Last Request (for additional transfer funds)
Paolo Nutini

3 He Said He Loved Me (but he wanted to move to a bigger club)
Reverend and the Makers

4 What Makes You Beautiful (is your ability to play anywhere across the back)
One Direction

5 Glad You Came (on a Bosman)
The Wanted

6 She Said (she would leave me if I didn't break my disc)
Plan B

Wake up Svein!

GUNPLAY, PENALTY SHOOT-OUTS AND DUKE NUKEM MARATHONS

Why working for Sports Interactive in the early days was a Boys' Own adventure

Paul: We used to play Duke Nukem Forever every day, and because we had this kind of small room with five of us, at the top of this old house in Highbury Corner, the other offices in the other rooms must have been like, 'What the hell are you doing? What is your business? Why is it booming?'

We sort of got a lot of childishness out of our systems at that stage.

Ov: It carried on to the next office, to be fair. Steering wheels on every desk. I can remember Ken the cleaner would come in and sort of whip round the bins, this kind of shadowy figure whipping round while we're killing each other with guns or driving cars.

Miles: And that kind of carried on until about six months before Paul got married, when his fiancé came into the office and took all the guns. We had a load of BB guns and that.

Paul: They weren't even game guns were they?

Miles: No they weren't, but someone had made the fatal mistake of pointing it at someone and

missing, and it hitting Camilla, and therefore she confiscated all of the guns.

Paul: It was part of the professionalising.

Miles: Camilla's not someone to argue with.

Ov: The sponge ball, don't forget that.

Miles: Yep.

Ov: The big sponge ball.

Paul: Oh we had some good penalty shootouts didn't we? That was in the office from '97 or '98 or something like that, wouldn't you say?

Ov: We'd have bike races around the sort of spiral staircase, and ducking as you went under, we had sponge balls landing in people's lasagne they were eating at the computer and splashing them, it was terrible.

Miles: And people working so hard they actually fell asleep at their keyboard as well. When Svein was over here, I've got a great photo somewhere...

THE NEXT BIG THING

Notes from the biggest scouting network in world football

From Danny Murphy to Eden Hazard, this team of volunteer researchers has been identifying the best young players in the world for almost 20 years. **Kenny Millar** found out how they do it.

Miles: Did CM even have real players?

Ov & Paul: No

Miles: CM1 had made-up data. CM2 was the first one that had real players, and that was the one with Neil Lennon and Danny Murphy, who were in Crewe reserves.

Miles: The research team was built organically to the point where we've got well over 1000 assistant researchers around the world now and 51 head researchers. We're at a stage where Everton licensed it off us. Whether they used it or not I don't know – that was very surreal.

But we have become very well known for finding these players early. It's not us directly that find them, it's because we have this amazing team of volunteers – in the main – around the world, who want their club and their country represented properly inside the game. That's where Messi would have come from; he would have been a kid they [Barcelona] would have just brought over from Argentina and he was in the game as someone who would become a future superstar. And we don't get many of the future superstars wrong.

Sometimes we do and those people have become quite big stories. People like To Madeira, who didn't exist. Or you've got Tonton Zola Moukoko, who was a really talented player, but had some personal problems, unfortunately.

£500-a-day drug addict was 'danger to the public'

JAILED FOR TAXI TERROR

A CRACK addict with a £500-a-day habit was yesterday jailed for nine years for robbing two taxi drivers at knifepoint in Northampton.

Justin Georcelin, 22, was branded a danger to the public and taxi drivers at Northampton Crown Court following a series of violent robberies last year.

He was also handed an indeterminate sentence, meaning he will be on license for life.

Georcelin was one of a group of addicts who terrorised taxi drivers in Northampton last summer, resulting in a shortage of night-time drivers and many private hire and taxi firms refusing to accept fares in the eastern part of town.

■ Full story on page 2

■ Jailed drug addict Justin Georcelin
Picture by NORTHAMPTONSHIRE POLICE

Ov: Freddy Adu?

Miles: Well, Freddy Adu could still make it.

Paul: And the Icelandic kid.

Miles: Sigporsson?

Paul: Yes!

Miles: Andri Sigporsson. Justin Georcelin is another one to look out. He was a 16-year-old kid at Northampton, who had a big career ahead of him and... I'll let you do the research on the story to see where it went wrong for him. It's also a fascinating one.

Ov: When I think about the research team, going back, we're talking about a time when we barely even had the internet. We used to send out printed charts of the squad, filled in with the ones we knew, taken from the Rothmans [the annually published directory of clubs and players in UK football]. Those would be sent out to fanzines to be filled out by hand and sent back. Some people would have accounts with Compuserve or AOL, so you would have a mixture of that and things coming through the door.

Miles: When I took over the UK research, half the people had email and the other half were being done by mail or phone.

Ov: That feels old.

Paul: There was a Norwich guy who kept sending us back pieces of paper with like, 18, 19, 20 everywhere.

Miles: We also had an Everton fan called Andrea who did the Cambridge research because she lived down there. Her stuff was absolutely spot-on.

Paul: Oh yeah.

Miles: Our Crewe researcher from that point is still with us, as well, the guy who first said Murphy and Lennon were going to be future stars, when they were in the reserves.

There seems to a buzzword for this: crowdsourcing. As if it's something that has been invented in the last couple of years. It hasn't. We didn't invent it. Anyone who collects stats works in that way. The internet just made it a lot easier. Crowdsourcing. We've been crowdsourcing for 20 years.

Paul: I remember going through all the fanzines, looking for ones that we could send to.

Ov: The response was brilliant. 'Someone wants me to fill in all these details about the team I know everything about'. These are guys who would go to the reserve matches and everything else.

Paul: What's that bookshop, the football one on Charing Cross Road? I went down there and I bought a whole bunch of stuff on Italy, Serie A all the way down to C. It had all the squads, the rosters, the history, all the finishing positions.

Ov: What's that bookshop called?

Miles: Soccer Scene.

Ov: Soccer Scene.

Paul: Possibly.

Ov: No, Soccer Scene sells shirts and stuff.

Paul: We bought these manuscripts – some enthusiast had just printed these out and sold them. You know, homemade folder thing. We bought these things and just typed them in. Where else are you going to get that information, before the internet?

Today, FM's 1000-strong army of researchers assess every player at every club on the game's database. During that time, they can see superstars in the making before any of the giants of European football are on the case.

We also had an Everton fan called Andrea who did the Cambridge research because she lived down there. Her stuff was absolutely spot-on

---

NEYMAR
MR NICE GUY

Paulo Freitas
Head researcher, Brazil.

I first watched Diego and Robinho in Copa Sao Paulo 2002. That's the country's main youth tournament, so it's always worth paying attention to. I'd heard of them both before as I'm a fan of youth football. I always check line-ups, results, match reports, goalscorers and, whenever possible, watch games too. The two of them were so impressive – Diego because of his class and Robinho because of his technical skills, though Santos were quickly eliminated in the group stage.

Later on that year, both of them were promoted to Santos' senior team, becoming their key players in the 2002 national title and attracting a lot of media attention along the way.

By then we'd already long since pinpointed their promise in Championship Manager.

A year earlier, Kaka was involved in the same competition, but he was a benchwarmer behind a player called Harison, so the press here barely paid any attention to him. Kaka finally made his impact at senior level a few months later, when he scored against Botafogo in the Rio-Sao Paulo tournament and from then on his career developed quickly.

Neymar was one that really stuck out, again in the Copa Sao Paulo. I first saw him in the 2008 edition. He was only 15, but he outshone much older players.

At the other end of the scale, Lulinha was one who didn't progress as we'd expected. He impressed me a lot at youth level, which is why he had such high potential ability in the game. He is probably the best Brazilian player I've ever seen in the Under-17 South American Championship, almost single-handedly leading Brazil to the title in 2007. Lulinha looked the complete prospect. He had great technique, with real pace and was a prolific goalscorer. Unfortunately, he just couldn't adapt to senior football. The pressure was too much for him to handle as Corinthians were struggling and he was the boy expected to save them. He couldn't do it and they eventually turned against them.

There's such a fine line predicting whether a young player will make the grade or not – even for a computer game!

*Paulo Freitas is Sports Interactive's head researcher in Brazil. By day he works as a lawyer, while he also contributes to Sky Sports and his own blog **http://ojogobonito.wordpress.com**. You'll find him on Twitter **@Cynegeticus.***

Neymar
Santos 2012

CERCI'S A JOLLY GOOD FELLOW

Alberto Scotta
Head researcher, Italy.

I'm very proud of the work we've done over the years with the Italian research. I say 'we' because, over the last 15 years, I've built up a fantastic group of assistant researchers that gave me a lot of accurate, detailed information about players – particularly the younger ones.

It's great to think that we've created players in the game who went on to do very well in real life, like Antonio Cassano (Bari), Giampaolo Pazzini and Riccardo Montolivo (both Atalanta) and Alessio Cerci (Roma).

Cerci, especially, was superb in Football Manager 2005 – he could play in every attacking position – and finally he became a great player for Fiorentina, and was close to signing for Manchester City at the beginning of last season.

I remember having many discussions with the other researchers over Zlatan Ibrahimovich.

When he came to my database he was only a decent player, while I was sure he was already a star – so I fought a lot with the other head researchers. His Current Ability rating was only at 130, while the likes of Alessandro Del Piero and David Trezeguet were at around 170. With those stats, he'd never play for Juventus, whereas in reality he was a first-pick for Fabio Capello. I remember someone saying, "His rating can be just above Yksel Osmanovski," but I fought to get him up to between 165-168 and, in the end, I'm pleased I was right about him.

The latest hot property we've created – who is becoming great – is Marco Verratti.

At the time of writing he's just been called up by Cesare Prandelli for his provisional 32-man squad for Euro 2012, even though he's a Serie B player. He was already a superstar in Football Manager 2010, when no one had heard of him.

I've had the chance to meet a lot of the famous players who are deeply in love with the game, like Massimo Oddo, Fabio Grosso, Ignazio Abate and Cristian Pasquato. Demetrio Albertini was another.

The funniest thing was hearing that Giovanni Trapattoni had asked Albertini for some information on the young England players before a match, on the back of the interview I did with him.

After 15 years of working with Sports Interactive, I feel so proud to be part of such a family.

The SI guys, the foreign researchers and all my assistants... I've met a lot of people through working on this game and some of them are now my closest friends.

I was addicted to and in love with their management games from 1992 and now, as the Italian head researcher, I'm even more obsessed with it.

CURRICULUM VITAE

NAME: JAMES WILKES

D.O.B: 6.1.1979

PROFILE:
I AM a young talented football manger with excellent communication skills with more than 18 seasons' experience in the professional game.
I score 20 on tactics, youth development and discipline and ranked as the best British and European manager of all time following my recent FAllcup triumph.

CURRENT EMPLOYER:
Jenkins Accountancy Services, Shepherd's Bush, London.

JOB HISTORY:
BARCELONA - 2008/2009 season
Taking over at the Camp Nou, I revolutionised their style of play. Using a radical 3-3-4 gung-ho attacking style we romped to the La Liga title and the semi-finals of the Champions League. But I felt this wasn't enough of a challenge so I took the Elgin City job.

ELGIN CITY - 2009 to 2013
Took Elgin City from the 3rd Division to the SPL before breaking the old firm duopoly of Celtic and Rangers to claim the double.

CAMBRIDGE UNITED - 2013-2020
Raised the mighty Us to the Premier League from the Blue Square Premier League! After seven seasons, lasting a total of 45 days playing time, I quit for a new challenge after winning the treble of the FA Cup, Premiership and Champions League - and successfully retaining all three the following year. Signed Lionel Messi to the club, among others

ACCRINGTON STANLEY - 2020-2030.
Having secured Champions League football for the first time in the club's history, Ihave made Accrington a football powerhouse. In talks to take Cristiano Ronaldo to the club on a Bosman. Won the FA Cup last season and missed out on my third consecutive title by a point to my old club Cambridge United.

REFERENCES:
I have saved all of my achievements onto my hard-drive and would be happy to forward you copies.
All of my Football Manager trophies (26 in total)

DELUDED: Game fan James

Crewe must be joking!

WANNABE SOCCER BOSS PUT PC FOOTY SIM SUCCESS ON HIS JOB APPLICATION

By JAMES CRISP

AN accountant applied for the vacant manager's job at Crewe Alexandra with a CV made up entirely of victories in a computer game.

James Wilkes, 31, sent a resume full of references to his trophy haul in *Football Manager*.

But League One outfit Crewe, who sacked boss Steve Holland on Tuesday, smelt a rat when they saw Wilkes' claim to have coached Cambridge United to the Champions League Final in 2020!

An insider said: "At first glance it was an amazing CV but when we took a closer look things just didn't add up.

"For a start, if he really had won the treble with Cambridge United I am sure we'd have heard of him. Likewise, if he'd broken the stranglehold of the Old Firm with Elgin City

"We gave him a bell and challenged him and he said he'd done it on Football Manager,

which meant he could do it in reality. He's not on our shortlist."

Sunday Sport caught up with the bachelor at his bedsit in Shepherd's Bush, London.

He told our man: "As far as I'm concerned I'm more than qualified for the Crewe job. No one can argue with my Football Manager trophy cabinet and I've spent the equivalent of a year of my life playing the game.

"I can't talk now. I'm in the middle of trying to sign Cristiano Ronaldo for Accrington Stanley."

WIN FOOTBALL MANAGER 2009!

SUNDAY Sport has 10 copies of Football Manager 2009 to give away.

The most addictive computer game of all time now boasts a brand new 3D match simulator. And you can get your hands on a copy, worth £39.99, thanks to our pals at Sports

Interactive and SEGA.

Simply answer this simple question: Who is currently caretaker manager at Crewe? Answers on a postcard to: *Football Manager Comp, Sport Newspapers Ltd, 19 Great Ancoats St, Manchester, M60 4BT.* Entries by Friday, Nov 28.

CURRICULUM VITAE

NAME: JAMES WILKES

D.O.B: 6.1.1979

PROFILE:
I AM a young talented football manger with excellent communication skills with more than 18 seasons' experience in the professional game.
I score 20 on tactics, youth development and discipline and ranked as the best British and European manager of all time following my recent FAllcup triumph.

CURRENT EMPLOYER:
Jenkins Accountancy Services, Shepherd's Bush, London.

JOB HISTORY:
BARCELONA - 2008/2009 season
Taking over at the Camp Nou, I revolutionised their style of play. Using a radical 3-3-4 gung-ho attacking style we romped to the La Liga title and the semi-finals of the Champions League. But I felt this wasn't enough of a challenge so I took the Elgin City job.

ELGIN CITY - 2009 to 2013
Took Elgin City from the 3rd Division to the SPL before breaking the old firm duopoly of Celtic and Rangers to claim the double.

CAMBRIDGE UNITED - 2013-2020
Raised the mighty Us to the Premier League from the Blue Square Premier League! After seven seasons, lasting a total of 45 days playing time, I quit for a new challenge after winning the treble of the FA Cup, Premiership and Champions League - and successfully retaining all three the following year. Signed Lionel Messi to the club, among others

ACCRINGTON STANLEY - 2020-2030.
Having secured Champions League football for the first time in the club's history, Ihave made Accrington a football powerhouse. In talks to take Cristiano Ronaldo to the club on a Bosman. Won the FA Cup last season and missed out on my third consecutive title by a point to my old club Cambridge United.

REFERENCES:
I have saved all of my achievements onto my hard-drive and would be happy to forward you copies.
All of my Football Manager trophies (26 in total) have been won without replaying any match.

I must be...
BUTTER

Djourou's smear tactics

By MATT PARKER

JOHAN DJOUROU has got a fruity secret — he loves smearing himself with mango-flavoured body butter.

The Arsenal star is not your typical rugged centre-half and when he is not rubbing himself down with beauty products...

London and eating them is pure joy," Djourou is addicted to computer game Football Manager 2009 and likes to cast himself as Gunners boss Arsene Wenger.

He said: "I am completely crazy about the game. I take it with me everywhere on my laptop. In this virtual world I can put myself in the shoes of my managers Arsene Wenger and the Swiss coach Ottmar Hitzfeld.

"But I don't always pick myself to start every game. I have to rotate my squad!"

The 6ft 3in star has won Swiss 20 caps and admits he is addicted to retail therapy.

He said: "I use my...

BLING . . . gold wearer Djourou

STAR . . . Djourou

Alberto 'Panoz' Scotta has served Sports Interactive for the last 15 years, improving with age like a fine Italian centre-back.

He's an interaction designer at Deltatre and worked on the London 2012 Olympic site.

Feel free to join his FM Facebook group at **www.facebook.com/panoz.fmitalia.**

In 2004, Alberto Scotta interviewed Demetrio Albertini before Italy played England. —————

AS: Tomorrow you'll play against England. Who are their best players in your opinion?

DA: I've played against Leeds in the last few weeks and they've a lot of great young players. I especially like Alan Smith and Olivier Dacourt.

Apart from that, there are obviously the very famous Manchester United ones, like David Beckham and Paul Scholes.

Yesterday the manager asked us about some young English players ahead of tomorrow's match.

Now I'll install the new copy of CM you gave me and we'll look at their stats together. I'll impress him with such a big and accurate database!

Cassano

Bari 2000

👓 FM STATS EXPLAINED

The key stats for players are Current Ability (CA) and Potential Ability (PA). With a numerical value of 1-200, the hidden 'Current Ability' (ie how good the player is now) score is the score that a player's attributes like shooting, pace, tackling, heading etc are weighted against.

The manager asked us about some young England players. Now I'll install the new copy of CM and I'll impress him with such a big and accurate database!

JUST SAY TO

Ze Chieira
Head researcher, Portugal.

I've spent some 18 years assessing players for Championship Manager and now Football Manager. Deco was my first real 'spot'. It was back in 1997 and he was only 20, having only just arrived in Portugal as another completely unknown Brazilian player. He was supposed to sign for Benfica, but during pre-season training they decided he was not good enough for the senior squad. Without even playing one friendly, he was loaned out to Alverca. They were a lowly Lisbon club who were deemed certainties for the drop from the Second Division, but that year they got a lot of players from Benfica through a feeder club agreement.

I was living in Lisbon at that time and taking my CM scouting tasks quite seriously because CM 97/98 was officially including the Portuguese leagues for the first time. I decided to take a look at him one night, through the pouring rain.

Deco, skinny and soft like so many Brazilian rookies, hardly touched the ball and I remember him being kicked all over the place. The new version came out just after that and he was rated no higher than an average unknown.

The good weather returned and Deco started to show his top quality – which is the phrase I'd use for someone capable of playing at the highest level. He'd established himself as a starter, but the media weren't sure about him. Deco was deemed too skinny, too selfish, too 'smart'.

I decided to have another look at him and I saw the best footballer who had ever played in that league. He was quality – everywhere on the pitch, with intuition, skills and pure magic.

Yes, he was skinny and clearly not a runner, but he had everything else to play at the very top level. I updated the database and thought, 'wow, people better get ready for the best prospect in Portugal'.

So when Championship Manager 3 came out in March 1993, Deco was programmed to be a future star. The database had been submitted way before he'd moved from Salgueiros - the smallest club in the Premier League, where he'd settled after Benfica had decided not to keep him on – to Porto. I got huge stick from the Portuguese fans complaining to SI about my supposed bias towards Porto, but I guess history has proven me right.

Of course, I could also brag about Cristiano Ronaldo, Nani or Ricardo Quaresma but, to be honest, those guys were impossible to miss.

To Madeira

Now this is a piece of CM history.

I was managing a growing scouting network, with more than 80 people covering almost every club in the country. Back then, the way the database was managed meant that only one researcher could work on it at the same time. There were different, but strict, deadlines for every research stage and some assistant researchers had trouble delivering their stuff on time.

I had someone offering to help with Gouveia, a club from a small town deep in the countryside, which is well known for the fine cheese rather than their football team. He claimed to know the staff very well as he'd been a player there in the previous season, before leaving to go to university.

He got his files and returned them on the very last day before the CM 01/02 deadline, when I was swamped with other entries at the same time. With little time, I had to make a choice, so I let the lower league ones pass with very minor tweaks. I obviously trusted my staff and their assessments. This is how a Championship Manager hero was born!

The researcher, Antonio Madeira, had created a character based on his own nickname.

Needless to say it was spotted almost as soon as the game came out, but it could only be corrected with the first data patch some weeks afterwards. The legend lives on to this day.

Fabio Paim

Fabio was a huge prospect, who was brought to the world's attention when CM4 was released back in 2003. He could and should have become a superstar, if only he'd kept his focus.

I was scouting for Sporting Lisbon during the previous season, so I got to know this kid very well. He'd been brought in from a small club near Lisbon and made a stunning impact at the academy with his unbelievable talent and flair. I don't think I'd ever seen another player with his natural skills in more than 18 years of scouting worldwide.

I still remember seeing him trashing Benfica on his own in a decisive derby match for the national under-15 championship. He scored three goals, with his last one coming after he'd dribbled around seven or eight opponents before literally walking the ball into the net.

He blew all of his chances with his off-field behaviour. At the time of writing, he's still only 24 and still looking for a way out of trouble.

Assistant Researchers

Since 1994, I must have had more than 1000 people helping me put together the various versions of Championship and Football Manager. Naturally there are a few stories along the way, with some of them putting their addiction before anything else.

A decade ago I had a very good assistant researcher who covered the lower leagues, at a time when there was very little public information available. The thing was, he made time by relaxing on his university studies – until he met a new girlfriend.

One day he came to me and said 'I have to choose between Championship Manager and married life'. What a loss to me. I hope he's still married.

Covering Portugal, Ze Chieira is Sports Interactive's longest serving Researcher – having started off back in 1994 before SI was even officially founded. Since 2001 he's worked as a scout for Sporting Lisbon, Vitoria Setubal, Academica de Coimbra and Panathinaikos. For the last two seasons he's been the senior scout at FC Porto. In real life.

Deco

Alverca 1997

IN GOOD KOMPANY

Kristof Terreur
Head researcher, Belgium.

I started working as an assistant researcher for Belgium in the late 1990s, after I'd discovered Championship Manager on a school trip to London. At that time, the head researcher was from the French part of Belgium, so I looked after all the teams from the Flemish area. I'd also manage the attributes of the youth internationals, so I'd identify young talents.

Back in early 2000, we started to establish talented 15-year-olds for the database. Although we hadn't seen these players live, we had a useful guide thanks to Belgium's main sports magazine Sport/Voetbal Magazine. They had weekly column dedicated to five promising youngsters and I came across information about the then-unknown Vincent Kompany.

The head researcher, Fabrice Leclercq, keyed in his basic details, but I remember we edited some attributes thanks to the content of the article.

It read: "Vincent Kompany is a right-footed defender. He is strong on one-on-ones, has good heading and an awesome tackle. His youth manager, Eddy Van Dale, adds that he also reads the game pretty well. He still has to work on his technique and his shooting."

At that time we didn't know what would follow for him.

Kompany made his first appearance for Anderlecht in 2003, almost at the same time as I started working as a journalist for Het Laatste Nieuws. I wasn't covering Anderlecht for the newspaper – I did KRC Genk and Lierse – but I immediately saw that article had been right, as did all the top European scouts.

I had my first contact with him in 2004 when he won the Golden Boot, which is the trophy awarded to Belgium's best player. He started like a comet at Anderlecht, but his career slowed down a little bit after a bad shoulder injury.

Kompany moved to Hamburg, where he wasn't as successful as he'd hoped due to injuries and personal problems.

When he moved to Manchester City in 2008, I covered one of his first games, against Chelsea. English clubs aren't so keen on newspaper journalists, but the City press officer gave me permission to talk to him for five minutes. The day after, he was on the same flight back to Belgium and we had a long talk, after I found him reading the financial pages of the newspaper. He's a smart guy!

From time to time I used to travel to Manchester or London to see him playing, but interviews weren't that easy to obtain anymore (aside from one with his sponsor, Nike) as he got famous and received too many requests. But we had a routine. After a Saturday game we'd fly back together to Brussels. He'd greet me warmly and we'd make small talk.

I must admit, I got goosebumps when I saw him lift that English Premier League trophy.

I'm so proud of the guy I discovered in a small football magazine article – and he still looks the same!

I have a really close relationship with Belgium's next rising star, Thibaut Courtois. I've known him personally since he moved from the Genk youth squad to the first team at 15.

I still remember his debut as a 16-year-old, when all the other goalkeepers were injured. The day before the game, the club wouldn't let me speak to him so I called his Dad. He told me that his son was jumping about on the trampoline in his garden – that's how relaxed he was!

Thibaut played terrifically against Gent, making some fine saves, and the night after that game I made sure to up his stats in the database!

I also recall him falling ill after that game. He puked and all the stress came out. Last year he became the regular first-choice, which was the beginning of a fairytale. He impressed from the first game to the last, making only a few small mistakes along the way. Since then I've interviewed him several times and what sticks out is that he doesn't feel pressure.

We kept in contact, also because I knew Tottenham and Chelsea were on the verge of signing him. I was on the front row of a transfer soap opera, before he finally moved to Chelsea, who loaned him to Atletico Madrid.

I flew over to Spain to watch him against Valencia. We talked afterwards, as we have done almost every week since – via Facebook, text messages and so on.

When I was promoted to chief reporter, he was one of the first to send me his congratulations – as I did when he won the Europa League.

If Chelsea's new £7million signing, Kevin de Bruyne, makes a name for himself you'll know who to call!

Together, our computer game dreams became reality.

Kristof Terreur is Sports Interactive's head researcher in Belgium. By day he works as Sports News Editor for Belgium's biggest newspaper, Het Laatste Nieuws. You'll find him on Twitter @elterror81.

Vincent Kompany

Anderlecht 2004

VINCENT KOMPANY
Miniem bij Anderlecht
Vincent, eerstejaars, is een rechtsvoetige centrale verdediger. Hij is sterk in 't één tegen man, kopt goed en beschikt over een uitstekende tackle. Trainer **Eddy Van Dale** prijst ook zijn degelijk speldoorzicht. Hij moet nog schaven aan zijn basistechniek en zijn traptechniek.

 **ANTHONY PILKINGTON** @Pilkington_11

Wow so shocked about the news that #htafc have sacked Lee Clarke! Top manager and did a lot for my career! #Gutted

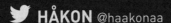 **HÅKON** @haakonaa

@Pilkington_11 I've done a lot for your career too. On FM11. You've played in two Champions League finals, and scored twice in the world cup

«Hij zal niet kraken»

Hij vond het wél best prettig, die aandacht op training. Maar zeggen deed Thibaut Courtois, 16 en morgen onder de lat bij Genk in de kraker tegen AA Gent, dat niet. Het spreekverbod dat Genk hem oplegde, weet je wel. Dus spraken coach Denier, keeperstrainer Martens en pa Thierry in zijn plaats. «Er zal geen scholierenkeeperke tussen de palen staan.»

16-JARIGE THIBAUT COURTOIS
MORGEN ONDER DE LAT BIJ GENK

KRISTOF TERREUR

tegen AA Gent, dat niet. Het spreekverbod dat Genk hem oplegde, weet je wel. Dus spraken coach Denier, keeperstrainer Martens en pa Thierry in zijn plaats. «Er zal geen scholierenkeeperke tussen de palen staan.

16-JARIGE THIBAUT COURTOIS
MORGEN ONDER DE LAT BIJ GENK

KRISTOF TERREUR

rustig. Maar hij vindt het wel leuk, die aandacht. Ik weet verdomd niet de verdedigers gezegd dat ze hem moeten steunen en helpen. Dat we het met een jonge keeper moeten doen, zou de gasten ook moeten motiveren. Dat zou mij toch extra energie geven.»

stamt ook uit een topsportfamilie. Pa Thierry speelde op het hoogste niveau volleybal en bleef in het keepersberoep.

Volleyballer

Courtois verscheen gisteren, zoals verwacht, niet op de persconferentie. «Pas na de match mogen jullie op hem vliegen, zei Denier. «Nu wil ik hem in alle rust laten toeleven naar de match.» Maar de aandacht, zoals die van de fotografen, deed hem wel iets, zegt pa Thierry: «Hij is erg

al komt die unieke kans veel sneller dan verwacht. «En die komt twee, drie jaar te vroeg, zegt Guy Martens, keeperstrainer bij Genk. «Wij haalden Casteels (andere jonge doelman, red.) en Courtois deze winter bij de A-kern om hen bij te laten leren. Ervaring opdoen in oefenmatchen ook. Niet trainbaar dus. Thibaut zal vrijdag niet kraken, daar ben ik van overtuigd. Zelfs al rolt er een bal door zijn benen. Hij heeft alles te winnen, niets te verliezen. 't Is een jongen waar je weinig emoties van kan aflezen. Een nuchter ventje, dat van thuis uit goed wordt begeleid. Hij

keeper in die klasse. We mogen hem nu ook niet over het paard tillen, maar af en toe zegt er wel eens een speler: toch een klasbak, die keeper. Thibaut heeft zich serieus ontwikkeld de voorbije maanden. Hij heeft een koene, snelle reflex, is een echte lijnkeeper. Een type Davy Schollen, al moet hij nog veel leren. Luka het goed op voetbalvlak, dan lopen de studies minder. «Sinds Thibaut bij de A-kern zit, kan hij nog nauwelijks de lessen bijwonen, zegt pa. «Hij volgt moderne talen in de Topsportschool. Vorig jaar was het kantje boordje. Ik hoop dat hij het nu redt.»

Courtois gisteren op training. Praten met de pers mocht hij niet, om hem in alle rust naar de match te laten toeleven. *Tyckers*

GUY MARTENS, KNEDER VAN TOPKEEPERS

Guy Martens (50) was zelf nooit een topkeeper. Sinds zijn 33ste is hij bij Genk keeperstrainer. Vooral de laatste jaren kneedde hij echte topkeepers: Bailly, Bolat, Verhulst en straks misschien ook Courtois. Een overzicht ja van zijn 'producten'.

- **Davy Schollen** (31, Anderlecht)
Op zijn 24ste bij Genk beland. Twee jaar gekneed door Martens.
- **Sinan Bolat** (20, Standard)
Van zijn negende tot zijn twintigste bij Genk. Evolueerde tot een halfjaar onder Martens.
- **Logan Bailly** (23, Mönchengladbach)
- **Bram Castro** (26, Roda JC)
Op zijn vijftiende bij Genk beland ... jaar onder Martens.
- **Davino Verhulst** (21, RC Genk)
Op zijn twintigste bij Genk. Traint nu ... jaar onder Martens.
- **Reed Boffin** (21, MVV)

THE POWER OF BABEL

Jeroen Thijssen
Head researcher, Netherlands.

Quite simply, Football Manager stole my life.

It is difficult to perceive how exactly, but it certainly has.

I remember playing several football management games in the early days on the Commodore 64, as well as on the PC. However, I am not sure I imagined myself sitting here many years later as a head researcher for Football Manager – never mind contributing to a book on the game.

Entire weekends were spent playing the game with my best mate, usually in the English lower leagues, while other teenagers ventured outside a bit more.

I've been responsible for the Dutch research since 2002 and I do it with great pride and interest. We have the important responsibility to make sure that game is as accurate as possible. This can be a challenge, especially if you are looking at young players that might turn out to be an absolute legend, or there are those that fail in their careers and fade into obscurity.

I had my reservations, or rather had to laugh, at the outrageous price Liverpool paid for Ryan Babel. But, to be fair, I also had my doubts whether Robin van Persie would ever even wear the Arsenal shirt in a league game. In my defence, he was not a model professional back then and not even the pro scouts get it right all the time. On the other hand, it's always fantastic to see the more unknown players in the game develop in real life too, and ultimately get picked up by decent teams. Kennedy Bakircioglu is a good example there. He had been great in several versions of the game, and wound up having two stellar seasons at FC Twente.

Several seasons ago I also regularly visited youth games at my local (and favourite) team ADO Den Haag. I was watching a youth game and was looking for some help regarding the youth prospects. One of the ADO staff asked me if I was a scout.

"No, Sir," I replied, "but I work for a game called Football Manager and I'm looking for more information on these youth players.

"Besides, I'm sure Ferdi Sonmez is on Arsenal's radar already."

I was invited into their meeting rooms as both youth team managers helped me with player names, positions and their preferred foot.

Sadly Ferdi plays in the amateur leagues these days. This scouting lark isn't as easy as it sounds!

Jeroen Thijssen is Sports Interactive's head researcher for the Netherlands.

*You can follow him on Twitter **@FM2013NL** or join **www.facebook.com/fmnederland**.*

LEO
AND OSKITZ

Ivan Abella Villar
Head researcher, Spain.

My colleague Nordin and I have researched Spanish football for Sports Interactive since 1997, so thousands of players have crossed our paths. Many of them showed great promise from a young age – some fulfilled that potential and others drifted away. Others caught us by surprise.

One we remember fondly is Xabi Alonso, because we started to track his development when he was very young.

Xabi had football in his veins. His father (Periko) won many caps for Spain in the 1980s, while his brother (Mikel) is also a professional, though not to the same standard. The other brother (Jon) is a referee.

He started in the youth ranks of Real Sociedad – a club that only signed Basque players or those from overseas. Working with a limited pool of potential players, it meant they had to look after the talented ones they did have. In their B team, or 'Sanse' as it's known in San Sebastian, Xabi played alongside Pablo Blazquez, who was a Championship Manager fan and helped us with the research of some Basque clubs.

It was 1999 and both players shared a room in the academy, so they were close – though we're still waiting for that Xabi shirt he promised to send! He told us all about Xabi and said he'd be the future 'No 5' of the Spanish national team.

In the name of objectivity, we treated his words with some caution, but before long he was in John Toshack's senior team and indeed captained them from an early age.

This is where football can sometimes be random and unfair.

In that same year, our co-researcher Blazquez was in Toshack's thoughts for the first-team, and he even warmed up alongside Javier Saviola in a match against Barcelona. He and Xabi were the pearls of the B team, but shortly after that match against Barca Blazquez suffered a serious injury that he never really recovered from. They'd been with each other every step of the way, but now one would go on to become a world champion while the other has been retired for more than six years.

Xabi was one success story, but over the years there have been others.

We first heard of Lionel Messi when he was 16 and playing in Barcelona's youth ranks. Our researcher there told us this tiny Argentinean could achieve great things in football, but that he was a bit small.

We first entered him in the 2004 database, under the name 'Luis Leonardo Messi' and we gave him a Potential Ability of -10 – the highest you can give. His Current Ability was only 65, but we adjusted that through the season as he gradually made his first-team breakthrough.

At the same time, we rated another player just as highly – Oskitz Estefania at Real Sociedad.

When he was 14, Barcelona and Real Madrid tried desperately to sign him, but he declined their offers to stay loyal to the Basque club. He was handed his debut at 17, before being loaned to Eibar, alongside an 18-year-old David Silva.

Sadly, in the following pre-season he sustained a terrible knee injury in a South Korean pre-season tournament and he's only played at a lower-league level since.

We honestly thought at the time he could match up to Messi, but I guess that's football. It can be a cruel sport – and that's reflected in Championship/ Football Manager too.

Along the way we've also made some memorable mistakes. In 2007, a Spanish player, Josu Sarriegi, moved to Athens to sign for Panathinaikos – who were known there as PAO. As we wrote the database, however, he accidentally became attached to the similarly named PAOK. Consequently, a famous Greek newspaper published an article making light of the 'surprise transfer'.

The most famous one we made was quite similar, but even more 'galactic' in its impact. In January 2007, Real Madrid were still in their 'Galactico' period when David Beckham opted to move to LA Galaxy. Once again, though, due to spelling mistakes we sent him a bit further – to Australia, and a lower division team called Adelaide Galaxy. The FM forums were flooded with complaints, to the extent that SI had to release a patch fixing the error.

Nordin and I even thought about making t-shirts emblazoned with 'I sent Beckham to Australia'.

Ivan Abella was head researcher for Spain from 1997 to 2011, and still translates the game into Spanish, alongside working in a bank.

Honorino Zamora – known as 'Nordin' in the FM community - has been involved with Sports Interactive since 1998. He's presently manager of a morgue.

 FM STATS EXPLAINED

Potential Ability is the score given to a player that represents the maximum ability he could reach if all things go well for him in his career (i.e. no injury problems, plays regularly, has a good attitude etc).

MICAH MAKER

Karl Barrett
Head researcher, Manchester City.

I've worked as the Manchester City researcher for Sports Interactive since the spilt from Eidos in 2004. During that time, I've created many young players of different nationalities who have gone on to play for City's senior side and represent their countries – including the likes of Stephen Ireland, Vladimir Weiss, Ched Evans and Dedryck Boyata. My two personal favourites, however, are from a little bit closer to home. Both have been capped by England and won major honours early on in their careers.

I first saw Micah Richards as a midfielder and he was so powerful pushing forward that I mistook him for an attacking midfielder. Indeed, in the first Football Manager, he was down as an AMC, something, looking back, that I got terribly wrong. This wasn't helped by me going to watch a City XI take on one of my local non-league sides, Stalybridge Celtic, in a pre-season friendly, when he scored a hat-trick in a 4-3 win for City. From that first glimpse it was easy to see that he was an amazing athlete who could bully the opposition with his pace and strength. I remember him not being allowed to take part in the first leg of the FA Youth Cup final in 2006 because he'd just established himself in the City first team. Without him, the back four just weren't the same and Liverpool cruised to an easy 3-0 victory.

He was brought back for the second leg and captained the side. With Richards restored to the ranks, it was a completely different City performance but they could only manage a 2-0 win despite completely dominating from start to finish.

He progressed to be a City regular and became England's youngest ever defender when he was capped in 2006. Now he's a City icon, having helped them pick up the FA Cup and Premier League title.

In that Youth Cup final second leg I mentioned, City's two brilliant goals were scored by Daniel Sturridge. I'd known about him from an early age, though it was a good few years before he was old enough to be included in the game. He made his first appearance in a January update and I'd armed him with the stats to become a very good young player. It wasn't long before people were posting about him on the SI forums, saying he was a hot new prospect on the game. A month or so after he was included in the game, I saw a report in the paper linking him with a move to Chelsea. Obviously, the Chelsea scouts had been playing Football Manager! He eventually made that move and now proudly possesses a Champions League medal.

*Karl Barrett is Football Manager's eagle-eyed Manchester City researcher. When he's not running his eyes over the stars of tomorrow, he works for a family-run electrical wholesalers. If you want to track him down on Steam to talk FM, his **gamertag is 'Bazry'.***

LOVE EM OR HATEM

Jerome Boudin
Head researcher, France.

For the last 10 years I've worked as France's Head Researcher for Sports Interactive and I've seen a lot of good players in that time.

I'm a Stade Brestois 29 supporter, so Franck Ribery is probably the most famous player I've seen before he became a star. I knew of his talent early on, but following his move to Metz in 2004 he achieved widespread fame with an outstanding performance in a 3-1 win over Marseille – when he laid on all three goals for his team.

Every Football Manager fan knows of Hatem Ben Arfa, who has been regarded a wonderkid in France since he was 12 years old. In 1999 he was selected to attend the prestigious Clairefontaine Academy. He was the youngest involved at the time and even featured in a television documentary which followed the boys' progress. A famous clip showed him having an argument with Abou Diaby. All of his coaches since then have praised his big potential, and I think we're now seeing confirmation of his great talent at the very highest level.

I regularly attend French youth tournaments, so sometimes see players who are a cut above the rest. Football Manager addicts should keep an eye on Wesley Said, who is one of the brightest prospects from the 1995 generation. The Stade Rennais FC forward first impressed me at the Montaigu tournament – a well-established Under-16 international competition – in April 2010 when he was a stand-out despite being one of the youngest involved.

*You can find Jerome Boudin at **www.frenchtouch.org.***

 FM STATS EXPLAINED

With young players, it's difficult to say exactly how good they will become, and so there are 'minus' potentials. The minus potentials - from -1 to -10 - offer a range of potential ability (PA) scores. For example, if you give a player a -6 then when you load up the game that player will be assigned a PA score somewhere between 90 and 120.

DIRTY SANCHEZ

Mark Hill
Researcher, Northern Ireland.

The joys of Irish football mean I have no wonderkids to speak of. However, I was once contacted, out of the blue, by a scout from a club competing in the Champions League asking after Jonny Evans – shortly after he was first capped by Northern Ireland. I loosely knew the scout through the Champ Man/FM scene but he was keen to know whether Jonny would be interested in a season-long loan to the continent. He wanted me to make the initial contact if I knew him. I didn't, but I was up for the challenge.

This was back in the pre-Facebook days, so Bebo was my first port of call and it all went downhill from there. Despite my best efforts to come across as professional as possible via social media, Jonny clearly wasn't too receptive as the next day he deleted his account.

Not one to give up easily, I then contacted his girlfriend via the same social network site - from memory I think I got a two-line response that again wasn't too receptive. Needless to say, Mr Evans didn't turn up in Europe on loan at the age of 18 and it was probably for the best, given his progress since then at Man Utd.

My highlight was probably an exchange with Lawrie Sanchez. I was in my first year of university and hadn't been looking after the Northern Irish research for too long before one day I got a call from Nick Habershon at SI Towers. He informed me that he had taken a call from the newly-appointed Northern Ireland manager, Lawrie Sanchez. Apparently Lawrie was keen to talk to someone about the Northern Irish data in the game.

I called and Lawrie answered almost immediately. I introduced myself and once Lawrie explained that a friend of his had suggested he utilise the Football Manager database as 'there's a lot of good stuff in there', what proceeded was effectively an interview.

How do you rate the players?

How often do we update the data?

What sort of contact network do we have established?

How reliable is it?

These questions were fairly straightforward and relatively easy to answer, which put me at ease, but it was the topic he turned to next that was key to the purpose of his call.

How do we know if a player is eligible for a nation i.e. Northern Ireland?

Lawrie was looking outside the box at this early stage for players who could qualify for Northern Ireland. Our problems at a national level were well documented, but some of our best players were the likes of goalkeeper Maik Taylor, who were not born in Northern Ireland, spoke with a broad English accent but qualified for 'our wee country' as the local faithful refer to the team.

I was stumped. This was a question I wasn't prepared for, but here I was speaking to the national team manager. Caught like a rabbit in the headlights, and trying desperately to sound like I had a clue what I was talking about, I said our 'contact network' were capable of finding out player eligibility. It was sort of true, at a push.

Lawrie said he was particularly interested in British passport holders and gave me a few names to investigate. The only one I can still remember is Calvin Zola, who was progressing through the ranks at Newcastle around that time. I was to get back in touch with him once I'd found solid leads to potential players. Needless to say, at 18, my scouting skills weren't the best and nothing developed from then on.

But as Northern Ireland rose through the rankings, beating the likes of Spain and England along the way, at least I was able to point to the famous name stored on my mobile phone.

"Yeah, me and Lawrie? We go way back."

*Mark Hill works full-time as a Football Consultant, compiling stats and player information for the betting industry and the IFA. You'll find him on **Twitter @FM_ Ireland** and **@markhilltweets.***

 FM STATS EXPLAINED

For a player to be given a -10 is extremely rare (there are only ever two or three players per release given that) and therefore when Messi was given a -10 it shows that the Spanish research team always had faith that he would become one of the great superstars of football.

MARK OF GREATNESS

Stuart Milne
Head researcher, Scotland.

If I was asked what the most challenging aspect of being the head researcher for Scotland is, I'd say it was the management of expectations. Before sitting down to write this I was shown the submission by Paulo – the Brazilian HR – as he talks about all the great players he's seen come up through the ranks in Brazil over the years: Kaka, Diego, Neymar and Robinho. And I sit here and think, 'Who have I seen come through in Scotland in that time?'

Kenny Miller? Wow.

Callum Davidson? Awesome.

Derek Riordan? Terrific.

The thing is, there haven't been that many great Scots that have come through in the 12 years I've been in charge of the Scottish research, but that's more down to players simply not living up to anywhere near their potential than anything else.

Every year I'm inundated with requests to make sure a certain player is given massive potential and ensure he's 'treated right'. So far for FM2013 it's Tony Watt. He scored two goals on his debut and so he must be destined for the very top of our game.

I ask, 'What about those that have come before him, like Mark Burchill?' But they reply, 'They were average! They were never going to amount to anything! But this Tony Watt ... he's the real deal'. It remains to be seen whether or not Tony Watt becomes the next superstar of world football. I could be doing him a disservice, but probably not.

Inevitably you get a certain amount of flak from people for not rating their favourites highly enough. I used to be accused of being a Rangers supporter by Celtic fans and vice versa. One even set up a petition against me. Then I confirmed I was a Dundee United fan and ever since I've been accused of overrating them, so there's no winning.

I'll hold my hand up to overrating Steven McConalogue, though.

He was meant to be such a good player back in his youth days. Sadly, whether it was his size, his Scottish diet or maybe even seeing how good he was in the game, he didn't come anywhere close to fulfilling the '-2' I gave him back in the day.

Of course, I can't mention the Scottish research without bringing up Mark Kerr. To most readers of this book, Kerr is a Championship Manager legend. You could buy him for almost nothing from Falkirk and he'd be a superstar for you, whether you were managing Burnley or Barcelona.

The thing is Kerr was never even rated that highly. He just had a combination of stats that the match engine turned into instant gold. His legend is as a result of a complete accident.

I can't even begin to tell you how disappointed I was when I actually saw him play for Dundee United!

Stuart Milne was the Dundee United Researcher from 1998, before heading up the Scottish data two years later. He's still searching for that elusive East Fife fan willing to help him out... You'll find him on **Twitter @SGMilne**

ROBBIE FOWLER Liverpool, 1999

"The whole club had been turned on its head in the summer, there were so many new faces I needed Championship Manager just to keep up."

In his autobiography, **ROBBIE FOWLER** recalls the pre-season of 1999, when Gerard Houllier, then Liverpool manager, oversaw a vast turnover of the playing staff.

FM at the Euros

ALAN DZAGOEV

The 22-year-old CSKA Moscow schemer was one of the breakout stars of Euro 2012, but he was old news if you were a fan of FM09. You had to shell out big bucks to land him and he could suffer from a surly attitude, but if developed properly his creativity stats soared off the chart. Three goals at Euro 2012 meant Europe's biggest clubs were finally in on the secret.

SACK THE BOARD

When Football Manager goes wrong

SI Towers is a big, slick operation. It still looks a lot of fun, but 20 years after the game was first released, the kids that created it are all growed up, and the BB gun fights, penalty shoot-outs and Duke Nukem marathons that were once part of office culture are no more. Every year, this studio reinvents the game and takes over the media and the market. Usually, it all runs as smoothly as Theo Walcott, but when it goes wrong, it falls apart like Owen Hargreaves.

CM3: WHO WATCHES THE WATCHDOG?

Let's begin in 1999, at an earlier incarnation of SI Towers. A phone rings and all the weight of the BBC and its consumer champion, Anne Robinson, comes down on the young men within.

Ov: Oh, did we end up on Watchdog?

Miles: Oh the Watchdog thing was brilliant!

Paul: Actually, sales took a rise after that.

Miles: We're the only people in the world that got slagged off on Watchdog and our sales went up.

Ov: I mean, I would say we were panicking then.

Paul: Was that CM3?

Miles: I think so.

Ov: There some nasty questions in there.

Miles: Well there was one. The reason it ended up on Watchdog, if I remember correctly because this was before I was full-time, so I don't have to take responsibility for this one... wasn't something changed at the last minute and it wasn't checked by our publisher at the time? So the discs went out and literally would not work on certain specs?

Ov: I don't think it was that bad, I think it was a sort of combination of people complaining about general crashes. I mean, there might have been something like that, it was pretty nasty.

Paul: It was pretty bad.

FMSML: WHAT HAPPENS WHEN YOU GO ON WATCHDOG?

Ov: Yeah, well we didn't actually appear on the programme, like, in person. It was like they got in touch with us – I think it was a fax, not even an email – saying, 'Here you go, we're going to put you on. We've had a few complaints about you. Would you like to make a statement?' I think we had a chance to say something, and it was really strange. I think we all ended up watching thinking, 'This is us, this is terrible'. You know, looking at the TV thinking, 'How bad is this going to be? Is this the end? Is this the sort of, you know, the final nail in the coffin for us?' But it turned out the majority of the feature was a build-up, like talking about the game, trying almost to promote it. There was a little bit at the end saying, 'Oh, a few people have had problems' and then that we'd already had a statement, or we'd fixed it, we'd put a patch out.

Miles: Yeah, the patch was out already.

Ov: We had a bit on the feature saying, you know, we'd responded quickly, we'd sorted it out, download from here. So it actually turned out quite well for us.

Miles: Not only did we do 'download from here', also there was a number given out to phone up, and you'd be sent it on a disc. It worked out all right in the end.

CM4: CRASHED OUT

With each game bigger and more successful than the previous one, SI aimed CM4 at a launch in the autumn of 2002. However, they were now producing a global bestseller with the same team and using the same practices as they had when they started out.

As the scheduled release date passed and then disappeared in the rear-view mirror, and with staff asleep at the wheel from overwork, the game was released six months late and with more bugs than the Watergate Hotel.

Miles: CM4 definitely came out with too many bugs; it was six months late when it came out.

Paul: Actually I think CM4 was one of the best lessons we had, because we realised when the game is just that big, we can't be this disorganised. We've just got to organise ourselves as a company.

Miles: And that's when I moved across full-time. I shut down the other things I was working on to come in and try and sort it out. But we were completely blinded on CM4, we'd been working on it for so long, and were so disorganised that we were doing 16-hour days.

MBE

OBE

Level of discipline:

20

Anne Robinson

Miles & Paul

Ov: But we massively underestimated what we had to do on it, and how long it was going to take. That's probably the biggest thing we've managed to improve on, being able to estimate how long something will take.

Paul: We rewrote CM to CM2, we rewrote CM3, so we thought, you know, another big update, we can rewrite. But the game had got so big by then. I can tell you, we haven't rewritten a thing since then and we're not going to. It's in a situation where we can do bits and pieces.

Ov: We rewrite modules each year.

Miles: We rewrite modules, and that's the biggest lesson we learned. But at the time with CM4, when it came out we did actually think it was good. We didn't realise how many bugs there were because we were a bit blinded to it, and as well as changing the production practices after that point, we changed the QA [quality assurance] practices as well.

Paul: We were just deluding ourselves through tiredness and exhaustion and hope.

Ov: We were six or nine months late with it weren't we?

Miles: Yeah six months late as well.

Ov: There was a lot of pressure from the publisher and rightly so. We'd said we were going to do this game a lot sooner and we just hadn't.

Miles: The stage we'd got to as well, it had become a running joke in the office, who could actually stay up the longest. Vaughany collapsed after about 67 hours straight.

Paul: Yep, and then we put a crash bug into it...

Miles:... I beat that, but I was hallucinating at the time. I was trying to get to 69 hours because I thought it'd be funny. At 68 I started to hallucinate.

Ov: At some point we'd twigged that you actually get much less done in that situation.

Paul: I mean also the fact people start settling down. In the old days, you start work at three in the afternoon and then you work till three in the morning. But that becomes less practical as things become more organised and bigger.

Ov: When we got more people.

Miles: To be fair, I'm in the office from noon, but I do work from home in the morning and I do still work till 3am a lot of the time, because there's so much to do. I like still doing it myself. I'm no good in mornings. Paul's here at 9am. We've all just adapted to how we each need to work as part of the team, and have an understanding of that as a team.

> We were deluding ourselves through tiredness, exhaustion and hope

Miles, Ov & Paul

FM09: RUNNING OUT OF STEAM

By 2008, FM combined the traditional disc purchase with an online authentication system designed to combat the widespread piracy problem that continues to hold back the game's year-on-year development.

Instead of getting ripped off by pirates, they were attacked by a new enemy, the hackers who went over the ball and studs-up on the new system, leaving gamers all over the world with a disc they could not use, and making the director of FM as popular as the chairman that sells Eden Hazard behind your back.

Miles: We introduced online authentication, and for whatever reason someone decided to do a denial-of-service attack on the authentication system, which was the third party company, the night before release. We'd had some dark days on CM3 and CM4, but that was the worst 72 hours of my life. I didn't go to bed for 72 hours, just trying to get people up and running and work out what was going wrong, and it was just a huge denial of service attack.

Paul: So basically people couldn't play the game, because you had to go online and register it all. Then they couldn't get online to the servers to do it, so they'd bought this box that they couldn't play. It doesn't get any worse than that.

Miles: It was just devastating, absolutely devastating, because we'd all worked so hard, it was the best game we'd ever made at that stage. I think FM12 beats it now, but death threats, everything under the sun. I think that's the only time I've had serious death threats.

Ov: You got death threats?

Miles: I get death threats most years, but that's the only time it was just about the game.

But I could completely understand why people were angry. Maybe death threats were a little bit too far, but I could understand everyone's anger. I was just as angry, for a start.

Ov: I think if you've bought the game and you can't play it, you can't start it, that's awful, but in a way it's worse in the past where, say, your game would crash, and you couldn't get it back. Then you've invested hours and hours in your team, and, I mean, what do you tell someone in that situation?

Miles: Well we try and fix them now, when it happens. We've been involved in this for quite a long time, but it's been quite a young industry and the tools at your disposal, in terms of games crashing, we're a lot stronger now, you have better programming tools. I mean, going back 10 or 15 years there were all sorts of mistakes being made everywhere. I think that hopefully 'saved game corrupted' is a thing of the past.

> I get death threats most years, but that's the only time I've believed they were serious

MORE THAN A GAME

How you have helped raise over £1m
for good causes by playing FM

Their logos appear every time you load your game up and they are on the
advertising boards around your ground, but how much do you know about
the charities that are supported and inspired by Sports Interactive?

**BEN KNOWLES, DIRECTOR OF FUNDRAISING,
WAR CHILD**

War Child help children and their families whose
lives have been disrupted by conflict. Their
partnership with FM has raised over £1m in direct
donations and in-kind support. That money goes
directly to working with children whose problems
extend far beyond which formation to use in that
tricky Champions League qualifier.

We met in the 1990s – I knew Miles in the music
days. War Child's first album was in 1995 and our
paths have crossed many times. I think he became
involved through Feeder.

The collaboration between War Child and
Championship Manager and now Football Manager
happened for three reasons. One, there was a
definite appeal for Miles in the work that War Child
was doing. It is a powerful and compelling cause
and has an amazing impact on children's lives.

Two, Miles and the team had an opportunity when
they were negotiating the new deal with SEGA and
they were keen to write in a charitable objective.

Thirdly, Julian at War Child and Miles are both
big Watford fans. In addition to the strength of the
cause, that helped. Personal relationships are
important in building the kind of relationship we
have. From the beginning it felt like a relationship
between two sets of individuals who were
passionate about the work they did.

It was never just about getting a cheque once a year. There was a huge amount of personal involvement in it. Miles, as the figurehead, became involved more than we could have imagined. Since 2005 SI have been the single biggest donator to War Child. We have raised over £600,000 from the donations and I would be astonished if the added value for us has not outstripped that.

We have a committee of people advising us on everything we do and Miles comes to that meeting once a month – we often host it at SI Towers. He has used his connections to help us in a number of ways, including our partnership with Guitar Hero.

War Child prides itself on our relationship with young people in a way that few charities do. Those organisations often view young people as apathetic, but nothing could be further from the truth. They just need access to the information and games have become increasingly influential in that. The number of hours a gamer spends in front of FM is more than the most dedicated music fan would spend listening to their favourite band.

War Child benefits over and above the donation we receive from every single game. Our presence on the in-match advertising hoardings is given for free and that's a click-through to the War Child website. In the months after release that is our biggest referrer by a long shot and we designed a landing page for people who come to the site from the game.

In 2009 we had a big project in Goma, in the eastern Democratic Republic of Congo. It was for street children, with no access to education, to give them the tools to create a future for themselves. This village was built on volcanic flow and these kids were playing football on volcanic rock, which is damaging to walk across. You wouldn't become a slide-tackling centre-back there, anyway.

We were raising money to build a pitch and buy equipment to keep them safe so they could learn the better parts of the game. That specific project was the one people saw when they landed from the game and that pitch has been up and running for a couple of years now.

People come up to me at functions and say, 'You're the charity that comes up on the loading screen for Football Manager'. That level of awareness is brilliant for us. People who play FM are people who run big business; they are involved in international policy making; they are high up in the music business; they are artists and celebrities. All these people tell us their awareness of War Child came through FM.

They have a committed fanbase within reach of their website and they are brilliant at telling these people about the work we do. That is hugely important for a small organisation like us.

People who play FM run big business; they are involved in policy making; they are high up in the music business; they are artists and celebrities

THE CONGO DIARIES ————————————

War Child invited Miles Jacobson to see the work Sports Interactive and the FM community supports in the eastern Democratic Republic of Congo. He blogged about his trip at **http://sportsinteractive. wordpress.com. What follows is a brief extract from that blog.**

Our first stop of the day was to visit a 17-year-old girl who is part of the independent living programme put together by Maison Marguerite to try and get the girls that they can't reintegrate with their families to become part of the wider society. It's a new scheme, and there are three girls currently set up in this way from Marguerite. The scheme itself has to be taken slowly, as it's not culturally acceptable in DRC for a woman to live alone.

The girl's story is quite hard to listen to, and she's only able to talk about it now because of the counselling she's had at the home. She describes still being alive as a miracle and, well, it is. She was 16 when the incident happened.

An orphan, she was living with her grandmother and there were a few family issues which she doesn't go into. One day, she was kidnapped, blindfolded, driven into a forest and thrown into a ditch where she thinks she was for a couple of weeks with no food, or water, just a couple of people guarding the hole. She awoke one day to hear a group of men discussing how they were going to kill her, but one of the guards was against this and when the men went away, he got her out of the hole, still leaving her blindfolded so she didn't know who he was; he ran away, but so could she.

She was able to find water to drink and some food in the forest, and walked for days until she found a road, discovering that she was in Rwanda. Determined to get home, she met a smuggler, and he helped her get over the border, where she made her way back to her grandmother's. When she got there, she was obviously traumatised, so was sent to Ngangi to get some psychological help, and started the cookery lessons there, whilst also attending school, before being moved to Marguerite.

Her grandmother wasn't interested in any kind of reintegration into the family, so the decision was made to put her into the independent living program. Initially, this was with another girl as well, but the other one couldn't cope without the safety net of Maison Marguerite, so went back.

The girl is still at school, and about to do her final physics exam. She's an obviously clever girl from talking to her, and speaks a bit of French as well as her native Swahili. She's also an incredible cook, giving us some delicious donuts, waffles and chapatis, which she sells when she isn't in school, and hopes to turn into a business (possibly with the help of the micro-credit system which I wrote about in the last blog).

Long term, she wants to become a nun to be able to teach others, although there was a slight irony that of the two posters on her wall one was of Jesus, one of a bunch of US rap stars, none of whose lyrics are exactly godly.

She's an inspiration.

DANNY LYNCH, MEDIA AND COMMUNICATIONS OFFICER, KICK IT OUT ——————————

Kick It Out began as a campaign called 'Let's Kick Racism Out of Football', a little after the first Championship Manager game came out. Since then it has pioneered a programme of education on issues around diversity and inclusion, the relevance of which remain undiluted 20 years on.

It was a fairly dark time for football in this country. The relationship came through Miles wanting to make a statement. Our logo is a statement. It was in their ethos. They are football fans with a social conscience.

We have found a way of educating the people who play the game on issues of diversity. That logo is a way in. We can use this opportunity within that community to educate about what is happening in our world.

Kick It Out was meant to be a one-off campaign but it gained so much momentum that we have become part of the football family; we're supported by the FA, the PFA, across the clubs and in their communities. And our working relationship with SI is an active one. The offices are 10 minutes apart. When we do forums, or when we go to grounds, people say they know us through the game. I don't think it's possible to quantify the value of that.

THERE'S ONLY ONE TONTON ZOLA MOUKOKO

The best footballers you never saw

In your greatest teams they stood shoulder-to-shoulder with Baggio, Shearer and Zidane. In real life? Not so much. We sent **Kenny Millar** on a mission to track down some of the legends of the game, to find out what happened to them in the real world and how much they knew about their iconic in-game status

ALEXANDER FARNERUD

Position: AMRLC

Real-life career: Landskrona BoIS, Strasbourg, Stuttgart, Brondby, Young Boys; Sweden (8 caps, 2 goals)

In-game high: Championship Manager 03/04

Unless you were content to play it safe in the hot-seat at a cash-rich super-club or fiddled with the Data Editor (not cool!), then you'll all be familiar with the tried and trusted recipe for success.

It's a simple model adopted by the likes of Porto in real life – scout, buy cheap, develop, sell big and reinvest.

Alexander Farnerud was the poster-boy for that kind of shrewd stewardship. Available for buttons from little Landskrona, the dynamic attacking midfielder's value would soar within a season.

Alexander, you were just a baby when you first appeared in the game...

Yes! I was only 17 and about to make my first-team breakthrough at Landskrona. I played Championship Manager at that point and in the game I'd already signed for Barcelona by the time I made my real life debut for Landskrona. Family commitments mean I don't get the same chance to have a shot of it now but for three years I was pretty addicted.

That seems a common phenomenon in Swedish football.

It's very popular in Sweden. Going right back, a lot of the boys in the Landskrona dressing room were right into it. It was the same when I made the Swedish Under-21 squad. We connected over a shared appreciation of Championship Manager. Then I moved to France with Strasbourg and one of my team-mates, Guillaume Lacour, said he

knew about me from playing the game. That was a strange experience, but I guess one of the positives from Championship Manager is that you get to know players often before they get their big break.

Did you ever cross paths with a certain Tonton Zola Moukoko?

I remember Tonton! He was with Derby County in England, but I knew of him from the Swedish youth international sides. I was in the age group below him and he was a very good player at that time. However, like a lot of young players, it can be hard when you go out into the professional game. Maybe he lost his way a little bit. My own career didn't hit the heights predicted in Championship Manager but I hope I still have time to play for a big club.

Tonton still attracts a lot of attention from his adoring fan-base...

No-one's ever really mentioned it to me. I guess I've missed out, but if people still know my name from the game then that's pretty flattering. I can understand their enthusiasm having played it myself.

Who were your team of choice?

I was always a Barcelona supporter so it was usually them. Thankfully, for a spell, I was good enough to justify signing myself. I'm not sure that would be the case now.

Farnerud

ANDERS SVENSSON

Position: AMC

Real-life career: Elfsborg, Southampton, Elfsborg; Sweden (130 caps, 18 goals)

In-game high: Championship Manager 00/01

The Scandinavian leagues are football's equivalent of the Playboy Mansion – packed with hot up-and-coming young talents eager for a chance to impress.

If you haven't scoured each and every club side for bargains galore then it's tantamount to gross negligence.

Anders Svensson was one such diamond in the rough. If you could tempt him from Elfsborg – and he didn't come cheap at around £500,000 – he'd blossom into the goal-scoring playmaker that every manager craves. The real-life version is back playing with The Yellow Ones following a four-year stint with Southampton, where he played in the 2003 FA Cup final defeat by Arsenal. Despite his advancing years, he remains a key member of the Sweden team.

Are you aware of your Championship Manager legacy?

Not at all. My big brother was always very keen on the game but no supporter has ever mentioned it to me. I have been playing it for the last couple of years, though, so I know how addictive it is.

Who gets the benefit of your virtual words of wisdom?

I play as Elfsborg as they're the team I'm passionate about. I finished third, then second in the League so I dropped myself to the bench and promptly won the title. I guess I'm quite tough as a manager! I'm getting on a bit now so after a couple of years in the game my stats start to drop.

The game seems to be very popular in Sweden...

I know a lot of players who are keen on it, especially in the national team. Our striker Tobias Hysen – who plays for IFK Goteborg and had a spell with Sunderland – has been playing it non-stop for years. He's been helping me out with bits of advice here and there, telling me who to sign.

Some of the world's best up-and-coming young managers have admitted playing the game kicked off their interest in coaching. Is that something that appeals to you?

Yes, it does actually. I wasn't something I thought about before I started playing Football Manager but, since I have, I've been thinking about it more and more. I find all the elements very interesting – signing players, coaching them and picking the team. It's something I'd like to explore further when I stop playing.

Any tips or tricks for our readers?

I don't actually sign many Scandinavian players, but I do always try to get the Danish midfielder Mads Albaek from FC Midtjylland. He's a solid all-rounder. I would also appeal to Sports Interactive to improve the ratings of the young players at Elfsborg. IFK Goteborg's players always seem to have good potential, but we have some of the best young Swedish players here so it's time that was reflected in the game. And it would make my job a lot easier!

Svensson

ROBBIE WILLIAMS

I got addicted to Football Manager AGAIN. They warned Ayda what would happen but I don't think she was quite prepared for what was to come.

Been on it day and night and the other day I decided to snap the disc because it all got too much. However (two days later) I re-ordered it on Amazon. It should come in the post tomorrow morning. Ayda will be thrilled!

ROBBIE WILLIAMS blogs in 2009, revealing how close he came to being part of the Football Manager divorce count.

PLAN B

*My biggest gaming moment was when I got Rushden & Diamonds into the Champions League after taking them from the Conference. It is so f****** sad to hear myself say that, but I love that game.*

*I love football, and if I'm destined to be a billionaire with loads of money, what am I going to do with that money? I'd love to invest in a s*** little football club and take them up the Premier League.*

PLAN B reveals the inspiration behind his next track – if only he could find a rhyme for Bakircioglu.

CHERNO SAMBA

Position: ST

Real-life career: Millwall, Cadiz, Malaga B (loan), Plymouth Argyle, Wrexham, Haka, Panetolikos, Samger FC, FK Tonsberg; Gambia (4 caps, 1 goal)

In-game high: Championship Manager 01/02

It's fitting that Cherno Samba's surname pays homage to the Brazilian dance and musical genre.

Quite simply – in our removed-from-reality-Champ-Man-universe – he's the closest football has come to replacing Pele.

Available as a prolific, precocious prospect from Millwall, the then-16-year-old could be carefully nurtured to achieve near-flawless striking stats.

He had it all – pace, power and pinpoint finishing on either foot.

Back on planet Earth, the once-sought-after teenager has enjoyed a nomadic career that's taken him to Spain, Finland, Greece and Gambia in search of football fulfilment, before recently putting pen to paper with Norwegian Second Division side FK Tonsberg.

You might just be the most prized player in Championship Manager history.

It's amazing to think people are still talking about this, 10 years on. No matter where I go, people recognise my name from the game and want to talk about it. It's bizarre, but it's followed me around since I was 16 so I'm used to it.

How does the in-game fame manifest itself in real life?

I've played abroad and walked into dressing rooms full of strangers, but a lot of them know who I am. That's been a good ice-breaker over the years. There can't be many people kicking about called 'Cherno Samba' so it's always good fun when someone realises who I am, usually in a shop when I hand over my debit card. I phoned up to get an iPhone upgrade and the guy on the other end of the line went crazy, talking about what a legend I was for him in Championship Manager. Thankfully it got me a good deal! That kind of thing happens quite a lot.

All positive encounters, we hope...

Someone set up an account pretending to be me on Twitter, which I think is a bit sad. I'd like everyone reading this to know that I'm not on there. I've been told he's even talking to journalists online, in my name. Everything else has been good-natured, thankfully.

You must have an army of full-time staff dealing with all this attention.

I wish! I try to answer all my messages but thousands of people still get in touch, from all over the world. I've had a few from Russia but there's only so much I can do when they're written in a foreign language. I listen to all their stories about the game but most of it goes over my head. I'm not much of a computer guy.

Do you think there's an argument that the hype hindered your progress?

No, I believe the opposite actually. My talent was maybe exaggerated but it has opened doors for me. It's up to me to work hard and realise my potential and I believe my time will come. Until recently I played with Samger FC in Gambia. Their Youth Academy is named after me, which is pretty cool. It's nice to put my famous name to good use. Now I'm with FK Tonsberg in Norway. It's an exciting new challenge. Who knows what the future holds for me?

Samba

FREDDY ADU

Position: AM/FRC

Real-life career: DC Utd, Real Salt Lake, Benfica, AS Monaco (loan), Belenenses (loan), Aris (loan), Caykur Rizespor (loan), Philadelphia Union; United States (17 caps, 2 goals)

In-game high: Championship Manager 03/04

It wasn't just the Championship Manager scouts that got carried away with US soccer sensation Freddy Adu.

At 10 years old his mother turned down a lucrative six-figure offer to join Inter Milan on the advice of agents. At 14 he became the youngest American athlete in 100-plus years to sign a major league team sport professional contract, linking up with DC United having been first pick in the MLS draft. Within the year he'd played and scored at senior level, whilst at the same time blazing a trail all over Champ Man 03/04.

He was no short-term fix, but the patient gamer would sensibly swoop for him on a free transfer and wait for him to be granted a work permit. After three or four years' careful nurturing, he'd explode on to the first team scene like a force of nature.

His flesh-and-blood alter ego initially lived up to the billing. At just 16, Adu was awarded his first full international cap, with a two-week trial stint at Manchester United coming not long afterwards.

His star was on the rise and he enjoyed the trappings of celebrity culture – with endless endorsements and a pop star girlfriend.

Despite the razzmatazz, though, he never really kicked on from there. Benfica handed him his golden ticket to European football in 2007 but a handful of appearances saw him spiral into a succession of ill-fated short-term loan moves.

Adu's currently inching his way back to prominence with Philadelphia Union and, with time on his side and a wealth of experience already under his belt, still has plenty of time to live up to his in-game billing.

Freddy, you're one of a rare breed that was well known to football fans prior to your breakthrough in Championship Manager 03/04 – even though you were only 14 at the time. Are you aware of the game and your impact on it?

Yes, I've heard of Championship/Football Manager but I've never played it. I first became aware of my in-game status from my fans on Twitter. They started telling me all about it as soon as I joined Twitter in 2008.

How do you feel about that? From an early age you've had to deal with a lot of hype but this is a different kind of attention.

It's great that all of these people all over the world are getting to know me as a player and as a person through the game. It's really helped increase my profile and the profile of American soccer in a different way to those who have been able to see me playing in person or on television.

Adu

GARETH JELLEYMAN

Position: LB

Real-life career: Peterborough Utd, Boston Utd (loan), Mansfield Town (loan), Mansfield Town, Rushden & Diamonds, Barrow (loan), AFC Telford Utd, Barrow, Boston Utd

In-game high: Championship Manager 99/00

Back at the turn of the millennium, 'the Welsh Roberto Carlos' could be plucked from Peterborough for a cool £80,000.

In the real world, the Boston United skipper is perhaps best known for being the inspiration behind Sky Sports' Soccer Saturday host Jeff Stelling's book – entitled 'Jelleyman's Thrown a Wobbly'.

Stelling famously commented, "Mansfield Town's Gareth Jelleyman has been shown the red card for dissent. Looks like Jelleyman's thrown a wobbler."

Wales have been spoiled with flying left-backs called Gareth. Were you conscious of your computer-based credentials?

My brother got me into the game. He told me I'd always end up captaining Wales and playing for someone like Real Madrid so naturally I was curious.

Who benefited from your tactical teachings?

I was playing for Peterborough at that point, so I took charge there. We had a good team with the likes of Matthew Etherington and Simon Davies and I'm ashamed to say I put myself on corner kicks, penalties, free-kicks – everything. And I was always captain. I eventually buckled and sold myself to Real Madrid for £20 million. It still rankles that I didn't hold out for more. In terms of signings, Tonton Zola Moukoko was my boy. He was brilliant playing in the hole just behind the strikers.

You wouldn't be tempted by one last shot at the game?

I've been working for a building firm for the last three years, so between that and my two kids my spare time is limited. I was sucked back into it in 2009 when I had a go with Barrow as I was on loan there at the time. But, after three hours, I'd only played one pre-season game. The game's moved on too much in my absence.

Any up-close encounters with the Champ Man community?

I'd often have supporters say 'Wow, you used to be great on Championship Manager. What went wrong?'. A few people ask for autographs and tell me how I've done in their game. I enjoy all that and you have to see it as a bit of fun. The strangest thing I probably every got was a letter from Sweden asking for a signed photo. The guy was a big fan of the game and said I was his main man. It doesn't get much better than that.

Jelleyman

FM VS THE PIRATES

Every year, Sports Interactive sell over 1m copies of the new FM release. However, the number of illegal downloads of the game are also huge.

Miles Jacobson blogged for Wired, the technology magazine, about the impact of piracy on 2012's FM app for Android.

Last week I found myself in one of those 'good news, bad news' situations. The good was that more than 100,000 people were enjoying the new Android version of our game. The bad news was that only about 10 per cent of them paid for it.

It went straight into the top 20 in many European countries, both in the 'paid app' and 'top grossing' charts, and a 4.4/5 rating. Which sounds like a pretty good start, right?

We created a handful of 'skins' for the game to cover the majority of devices resolutions. Once a player has installed the game on their phone, the handset senses which resolution the phone can handle and downloads the appropriate skin.

As our sales passed the 10,000 mark, I asked to see the figure for skin downloads... it was up to 113,000. Because every installed copy of the game – legitimately bought or not – needs a skin, we were able to make a pretty direct comparison between our sales figures and our actual user base.

I tweeted about this 9:1 piracy ratio, calling those that had bombarded us with requests for the game and then pirated it 'dicks'. I make no apology for this. Anyone who illegally downloads software is a dick.

My tweet was picked up by a few news outlets, and I watched the comments sections with interest. Most were from people shocked at how high the ratio was, but there was also a handful of piracy apologists claiming that the game is too expensive (which is no excuse for illegal downloading - games are entertainment, not a human right), that it is not available in some countries (for legal reasons out of our hands), that the game should be free to play (not possible with our current licensing arrangements) and the argument that we don't lose anything from piracy, so what does it matter?

Piracy is a fact of life for game developers. I'm not stupid enough to think that 100 per cent of pirated games are lost sales - there are, of course, some people who would not buy or play a game if it wasn't available for free, but there are also some dishonest people who pirate things they would otherwise buy, just because they can.

The thing is, people who make games do lose from piracy. We lose from the small per cent of pirated copies that are lost sales, but we also have direct costs, both financial and 'opportunity costs', which can be attributed to every version, pirated or not. Whether that be server costs (for skin downloads), support costs (believe it or not, pirates still ask for customer support) and wasted time trying to deal with it all.

This is an edited version of a blog that appeared in Wired magazine, 2012

JOAO PAIVA

Position: ST

Real-life career: Sporting CP, Sporting B, Maritimo B, Espinho, Apollon Limassol, AEK Larnaca, Luzern, Grasshoppers Zurich

In-game high: Championship Manager 01/02

Championship Manager 01/02 was a vintage year for cheap, prolific Portuguese strikers.

While phantom frontman To Madeira is the stuff of legend, he was no more a must-buy than 17-year-old Sporting Lisbon wonderkid Joao Paiva – available, beautifully, for a nominal fee.

What did Championship Manager mean to you?

A lot! I know the game very well. I played it a lot when I was younger.

Who was your team of choice?

I remember in one of the early editions you didn't have as many teams to choose from, so first of all I managed Manchester United. But my real team was Wimbledon. When the Portuguese teams came in I'd play as Sporting Lisbon so I could coach myself.

You were a goal machine in Champ Man 01/02...

My main attribute in the game was high finishing statistics, and I always thought that was true in real life too. I don't need many chances to score. At the time I was one of the most promising players in the Sporting Lisbon youth set-up alongside Cristiano Ronaldo and Ricardo Quaresma. I was the top scorer from an early age and I'd been capped at the various age levels for Portugal. I don't know how the people behind the game judge the players but I can see why they rated me highly at that point.

Who made you aware of your in-game prowess?

My brother, initially. He was a big Sporting fan so it

was a bonus I was already in their ranks. I scored a lot of goals for him too! Gradually more and more people mentioned it, and one memory sticks out.

Go on...

When I was 17 I travelled with the Sporting squad for the first time, for a friendly match against a Second Division team in the north of Portugal. One small boy from the village came up to the group of players and asked to see me. Remember I was an unknown, in the company of established names like Mario Jardel and Sa Pinto. He said I was the best player in Championship Manager but that he'd signed me for Benfica – the rivals! It gave the other players present a good laugh.

Did that kind of thing happen a lot?

It started happening a lot, especially at away games. I've had many more messages since the explosion of Facebook. People will get in touch to ask for a signed picture or shirt. In the last year that's happened around 25 times.

So the interest has followed you around for the best part of 10 years now?

I didn't know how much global appeal there was until I moved to play in Cyprus, where a lot of people wanted to talk to me about it. I understand the interest because I loved the game myself. The only downside was not being able to fulfil my computer game potential in real life.

Paiva

JOHN WELSH

Position: D/DMRLC

Real-life career: Liverpool, Hull City (loan), Hull City, Chester City (loan), Carlisle Utd (loan), Bury (loan), Tranmere Rovers, Preston North End

In-game high: Championship Manager 99/00

French midfield fire-fighter Claude Makelele was regarded as football's ultimate defensive midfielder.

But long before he strutted his stuff at Stamford Bridge, John Welsh was bossing the Champ Man scene.

Equally dependable in a variety of positions, the former real-life Liverpool reserve captain and England Under-21 starlet was the sort of man's man you could rely upon.

In the summer of 2012 John moved from Tranmere Rovers to Preston North End.

Welsh

It's said Chuck Norris once cowered from a 50-50 with you, John. How much do you know of your Champ Man alter ego?

I've been a big, big fan of the game for as long as I can remember. I used to stay in to play it with my mates and I still buy it every year without fail. It's a bonus that I was half-decent too. At the time reporters would often tell me about their saved games over the course of an interview. Even now I still have supporters, particularly at away games, mention it. They'll tell me I got 50-odd caps for England and ask what I'm doing playing in League One.

Who do you take charge of when you don that make-believe manager's jacket?

I'm a big Liverpool fan so it's usually them. Back in the day I'd work myself into the team and put myself on penalty duty to boost my goal tally. I got more opportunities than I deserved on the game and I never considered selling myself. Not once. I've managed Barcelona and tried lower league challenges for a while but I get frustrated with a lack of transfer funds. Once I was managing Tranmere on the bus to an away game. The lads sitting round about me were after virtual pay rises and I got dogs' abuse for ditching Tranmere to accept a Premier League job offer. We've got quite the Football Manager community going at the club and it's perfect for those long-haul road trips. We're always giving each other tips on who to sign.

Any top tips?

It sounds simple but it's worth taking the time to look for the best young players. I remember getting a lot of joy from Billy Jones at Crewe and Phil Jones at Blackburn, though I tend to steer clear of the over-priced English market. And there's no room for sentiment. I've given up on signing myself.

JUSTIN GEORCELIN

Position: ST

Real-life career: Northampton Town

In-game high: Championship Manager 01/02

Sadly, not all of our 'Tonton' players achieved footballing fulfilment.

Justin Georcelin was a gifted goal-scorer as he rose through the ranks at Northampton Town – blessed with raw talent that was reflected in the much-heralded 01/02 version of the game.

However, life doesn't always go to plan, and he was tackled far harder by his own demons than any centre-back ever could.

Without even having played a first-team game for the Cobblers, his football career was left in tatters by a dependency on drugs.

■ **Jailed drug addict Justin Georcelin**
Picture by NORTHAMPTONSHIRE POLICE

A club source revealed he'd set his sights on pursuing his athletic ambitions in America but that was a non-starter.

Sucked into a downward spiral, he fell in with a bad crowd and became increasingly desperate in his bid to fund a £500-a-day crack habit.

On March 9, 2006 Georcelin was jailed for nine years – with a minimum term of four and a half years – for robbing two Northampton-based taxi drivers at knifepoint. He was only 22 years old.

The attacks were so gruesome that local taxi firms refused to accept fares from the east side of town.

Georcelin has since been released from prison and has a second chance at achieving something meaningful from life.

But it won't be on a football field.

KENNEDY BAKIRCIOGLU

Position: AM/FRLC

Real-life career: Assyriska, Hammarby, Iraklis, Twente, Ajax, Racing Santander; Sweden (14 caps)

In-game high: Championship Manager 3

Quite simply, Kennedy Bakircioglu is a stick-on for the Champ Man Hall of Fame. He racked up assists and goals with effortless ease, no matter where you deployed him.

In the summer of 2012, Kennedy looked like he was on his way out of Racing Santander.

How does it feel to have one of the most famous names in Championship Manager history?

It's fantastic! For the last 10 years now people have mentioned me in relation to the game – friends, team-mates and complete strangers.

Give us an example...

I remember, when I was still at Hammarby, travelling to play a game against SK Brann in Norway. After the match one of their players approached me on the pitch and told me what a good player I was for him in the game. That kind of thing happened from time to time. I also recall some people saying I'd refused to sign for their team so I must have been picky about my clubs! I started to play the game myself after hearing that.

You went on to play for some pretty big clubs – and they don't come much bigger than Ajax. But is it fair to say you made your name through the game?

My problem was that I stayed in Swedish football for a long time. If I'd left earlier people may have known about me for more than just Championship Manager. But the way football works you don't always get what you deserve and my chance didn't come until later on.

What about your trial at Manchester United?

Yes, I trained with them for a couple of months when I was 17. It was a dream come true. I'd train with their first team and play with the second string. It was at a time when their squad was packed with big names like David Beckham, Paul Scholes, Ryan Giggs, the Neville brothers, Dwight Yorke and Teddy Sheringham. They had Jaap Stam, too, who I later played with again at Ajax.

Did it inspire you to step into Sir Alex Ferguson's shoes in the game?

It did actually. They were always a team I admired anyway and, in particular, I admired David Beckham as a player. So after the trial I managed them and signed myself. It was a case of what might have been. I played in the middle, pushing Beckham out right. I let him take the odd free-kick – he is the master after all. His crosses made me look even better in the game.

Any other team take your fancy?

Other than United, the ones that stick out are Inter Milan and Barcelona. I remember signing myself for Barcelona and thinking it was great to see me in their squad – even though it was only a computer game. I played myself in the number 10 position, shunting Ronaldinho out wide to make way. It worked a treat.

Bakircioglu

LIONEL MORGAN

Position: AML

Real-life career: Wimbledon

In-game high: Championship Manager 03/04

Had his career not been cruelly cut short by injury, there's every chance Lionel Morgan's real-life career would have mirrored his explosive impact on the Champ Man 03/04 scene.

A pacey left wing prospect, Morgan was an essential signing – even for the cool £1million demanded by a stubborn Wimbledon.

Sadly he was forced into retirement at 21 years of age after sustaining a 'bruised and lacerated ankle' courtesy of a Tim Sherwood tackle in January 2003 from which he never fully recovered – almost a year to the day after Tottenham had had a £750,000 bid for him knocked back.

Spurs had an offer accepted in June 2003, but Morgan failed the medical and was eventually forced to concede that he wouldn't make it back to the same level he was at prior to the knock.

Having experienced the highs and lows of professional football, even at such a tender age, he's now putting that to good use.

In 2011 he established a player management company, Infinite Sports Management, with his friend and former team-mate, Jobi McAnuff.

Before there was Lionel Messi, there was Lionel Morgan...

I do get people asking if I'm THE Lionel Morgan from Championship Manager quite a lot. I was addicted to the game myself so that doesn't come as a shock. The one thing that's a bit weird is when Wimbledon fans I talk to on Facebook compare my real life football career to my in-game one. I remember one fan sending me a picture they wanted signed. Stuck to the back was a print-out of my Championship Manager stats, which was quite funny.

Did you ever mentor your virtual mini-me?

Funnily enough I never used Wimbledon as me team and I never even bought myself, until friends began advising me to do so because I turned out to be one of the best players in that version of the game. I'm an Arsenal fan so I'd usually go them. My ultimate signing was probably Anatoli Todorov, the young Bulgarian striker. After half a season in the reserves he'd blossom into a guaranteed 25-goals-a-season man. I can vouch for the people who say they can lose all track of time when they're immersed in it. Two hours would disappear and you hadn't even started the season.

It wasn't a waste of time, though, was it?

Not at all! I actually got a job with Opta on the back of the game. The guy who interviewed me was a massive man of the game and it definitely helped secure me the gig. It was based around tats and recording them live. I remember, in that interview, that the guy was talking about football and I mentioned playing the game. That's when he clicked and remembered my name from Championship Manager. The whole tone of the chat changed from there on in. I was there for a season and most people in the company were Champ fans. It was that sort of age group. I managed to a friend a job there – after he put Championship Manager on his CV!

What does the future hold for you?

Since leaving Opta, I worked as a coach and for the Press Association. I've set up my own football agency with Jobi McAnuff and we also have our own academy, nursing young talent and then putting on showcase matches for them against professional teams. The aim is to get them a contract. I still get little reminders of the past. I played in a football tournament at the Emirates recently. One of my team-mates said he'd like to see how accurate these Championship Manager 03/04 stats were. Fortunately he said it was reliable enough – apart from my fitness, which he'd have scored five out of 20!

Morgan

THE ONES THAT GOT AWAY

Believe it or not, tracking these legends of our time wasn't a seamlessly smooth process.

We were met with a wall of silence from the first player we asked to take part – former Manchester United striker Alex Notman, who was last spotted playing for Scottish Highland League outfit Formartine United.

The vast majority of those we approached were only too happy to tell their own, unique Champ Man/FM stories but a frustrating few proved elusive.

Despite the best efforts of the Belarusian FA, the shy and retiring Maxim Tsigalko couldn't be coaxed into a chat.

We hit dead ends with media shy Ivorian hit-man Ibrahima Bakayoko and Icelandic goal machine Andri Sigporsson.

If anyone's interested, the latter now helps run his father's bakery in Iceland but isn't 'the type' to discuss these trivial matters according to a source close to him.

Two Premier League clubs refused to have anything to do with the book, citing sponsorship deals with a rival video game company who blew the chance to take on Championship Manager back in the day.

And 'the people' surrounding one inconsistent Russian playmaker recently loaned from Arsenal to Zenit St Petersburg, who will remain unnamed, uttered the immortal line 'Andrey doesn't do anything for free'.

Rest assured, if an in-game legend isn't featured in this chapter it wasn't for the want of trying.

MARK KERR

Position: CM

Real-life career: Falkirk, Dundee Utd, Aberdeen, Asteras Tripolis, Dunfermline

In-game high: Championship Manager 01/02

Truly the stuff of legend, Mark Kerr was the best £40,000 you'll ever spend.

Whatever your budget, whatever your level, the Scotsman was the perfect blend of craft and graft in the midfield engine room.

Kerr carved out a more than respectable career in Scotland's top-flight, in addition to a short stint in Greece.

Renowned for his composure and range of passing, he's most recently been pulling the strings for Dunfermline.

When did you first realise you were a Champ Man legend?

I was just coming through the ranks at Falkirk when it all kicked off, so I could only have been about 17 or 18. My friends were all mad on it and let me know pretty quickly that I was half-decent.

'Half-decent' doesn't really do it justice. Did your in-game fame transfer to the real world?

It was pretty crazy for a year. I did an interview about it for Match magazine back in the day. And when I won Young Player of the Month I'd have people from computer magazines or the game itself up asking questions. Supporters mention it to me all the time, wherever I go, but there's been nothing too weird thankfully.

Any fanatics stick out?

I saw an interview with the comedian, Kevin Bridges. He talks about winning the Champions League with Borussia Dortmund against AC Milan – and I scored the goal. I posted that on my Facebook Wall. That did make me laugh. I mean, it's Kevin Bridges! The man's a legend.

When Portuguese striker Pedro Moutinho signed for Falkirk his only previous knowledge of the club was from signing you in CM. Any similar stories to share?

It's funny hearing that, because in 2010 I moved to Greece to play for Asteras Tripolis. I walked into a new dressing room, not knowing anyone, but it turned out a good few of them knew who I was – just from Champ Man. It's weird to think I've got that kind of profile from a computer game.

OK, Mark, time for the biggie. Did you play the game yourself?

I'm sorry to say that I never really got into it. I did play for a while at Aberdeen, when a few of the lads were obsessed with it, but never really got the bug. Maybe I'll have more time for it when I hang up my boots.

Kerr

MICHAEL 'MIKE' DUFF

Position: D/DMR

Real-life career: Cheltenham Town, Cirencester Town (loan), Burnley; Northern Ireland (24 caps)

In-game high: Championship Manager 97-98

Michael Duff is right-back royalty.

The Guardian's Rob Smyth, in a feature entitled 'The Joy of Six: great Championship/Football Manager players', described Duff perfectly as "The model pro. Mr Reliable. Gary Neville without the shop stewardry and bumfluff moustache. Cafu without a free bus pass."

We gamers know you better as 'Mike'...

Every match programme and stadium announcer calls me Mike, whereas I've always called myself Michael. My Mum asks why that is. I blame the game!

Ah, yes, 'the game'. Were you aware you were Cheltenham's cyber Cafu?

It all kicked off around 1998, and then I remember doing an interview with Championship Manager's magazine for their 10-year anniversary. I cost around £50,000 and always ended up at one of the big teams. I reckon I could walk down any street un-noticed, but so many people will know me through Champ Man.

Do you play?

Five or six of us at Burnley are hooked. We fire up the iPads and trade tips, especially those of us managing in the lower leagues. I knew I was in deep when I was watching Sky Sports News and knew all about a young Middlesbrough striker, Jonathan Franks, who had just gone on loan to Yeovil – purely because I'd signed him in the game.

Talk us through your memorable managerial quests.

I won the Champions League recently with Atletico Madrid, but it got to 2024 and I'd been unbeaten for 65 games so I started again with Nuneaton Borough. There I discovered an Icelandic regen at Forest Green Rovers, who cost £100,000 and is now worth £28 million. In terms of 'real' players I'd recommend Jack Robinson at Liverpool.

What about the ever-reliable 'Mike' Duff?

Sadly I'm not very good on the latest version. I flogged myself to Ipswich but it's fine – the virtual 'me' earns more money there than I do in real life.

What's this about you stalking poor Ishmael Miller?

We played Nottingham Forest in January 2012 and at the time I was managing them in the game. I'd been telling my room-mate, Dean Marney that I'd take the chance to personally thank Ishmael Miller for his five years of non-stop goals that propelled me to the Premier League title. The game stopped when someone got a head knock and I took my chance. Dean was in stitches as I told Ishmael that he'd done unbelievably well for me. He didn't have a clue what I was talking about at first but then said 'It's a shame it's only a game – I'm s*** in real life'.

Duff

MICHAEL DUNWELL

Position: ST

Real-life career: Hartlepool, Norton & Stockton Ancients, Billingham Synthonia, Durham City, Bishop Auckland, Billingham Town

In-game high: Championship Manager 01/02

Lower league gamers will appreciate that every penny is a prisoner – and you can't gamble a season's budget on a Champ Man also-ran.

Thankfully hot-shot hitman Michael Dunwell was a sound investment, costing around £300,000 from those tough-as-teak negotiators at Bishop Auckland.

Nowadays he leads the line as player-assistant manager at Northern Football League Division One outfit Billingham Town.

Does this Champ Man celebrity status come as a shock to you, Michael?

I played the game, so I remember there was a bit of chat about it at the time. If I remember rightly I was at my virtual reality peak for Bishop Auckland. I was really cheap and scored lots of goals. If you didn't have much money to spend, I was your man.

Did you splash out to buy yourself then?

No, I wasn't that bad. I never once signed myself and I've managed to wean myself off the game since then.

Does that mean you've left your double life behind?

Not quite. As well as playing and being assistant manager at Billingham Town I manage a mail order company called Decorating Direct, in Middlesbrough. My boss ran my name through a search engine and all the responses were about Championship Manager. He didn't know he had a computer game legend amongst his ranks.

It's embarrassing to admit, but I Googled myself a couple of years ago and it was fun to read through some of the mentions.

So have any dedicated diehards made the pilgrimage to watch Billingham Town?

Not that I know of, but I've had opposition players say they've had me on their books. One lad had me partnering Robbie Fowler up front for his Liverpool team and apparently we were quite a prolific pairing. Sadly that didn't translate to real life.

How do you feel about this lasting legacy offered by Championship Manager 01/02?

I've never seen it as a hindrance. It's just a bit of fun and, in a way, it's nice. I only played professional football for about three minutes, when I came on for Hartlepool in 1999 away at Southend. So it's strange to think people know who I am through the game.

NII LAMPTEY

Position: AMRLC

Real-life career: Anderlecht, PSV, Aston Villa, Coventry City, Venezia, Union Santa Fe, Ankaragucu, Uniao Leiria, Greuther Furth, Shandong Luneng, Al-Nassr, Asante Kotoko, Jomo Cosmos; Ghana (38 caps, 8 goals)

In-game high: Championship Manager 93/94

History may judge Nii Lamptey as the perfect example of a football prodigy who crashed and burned under the weight of expectation – after all, Pele himself said 'Lamptey is the new Pele'.

But that doesn't do the Ghanaian's incredible journey justice.

Overcoming a particularly troubled childhood, he found solace at a Muslim football camp, where he had to convert to Islam to qualify. His talent took him to Europe, initially with Anderlecht, before he embarked on a nomadic career – never quite fulfilling his early potential but, at the same time, living a dream that must have seemed a distant one in those difficult early years.

Have you even heard of Championship Manager?

Yes! I recall on one particular trip to Europe in the 90s that someone first mentioned it to me. I can't remember exactly who it was but I was told how big I was in the game.

So you were aware of your legendary status?

Yes, yes. Some people have told me that they rarely lost games whenever they had me in their team. That was a nice thought. I was not really a computer person back in the day so I didn't get any fan-mail as such, but sometimes on very random occasions people mention how much they liked me in the game.

Did you ever get a chance to play the game yourself?

[Laughs] Not at all. Maybe if I get my kids back in time they can play!

What are you doing with yourself these days?

I'm into business and venture into areas that I think are commercially viable. I also run a school with my wife, called GlowLamp International. Cattle-farming is not a full-time business that I am into but, yes, I've ventured into it now and again when it has looked good. Football-wise, of course I am still involved. The game is very much a part of me. I help a few kids to join education with football so that they don't fall into the hands of exploitative people. I also do scouting now and again.

Can you think of a reason why you were so big on Championship Manager?

Well, in the early 90s, people expected big things from me and I'm quite sure that was the reason. Whoever made the game will have taken that chance in the hope that if I become a big name, the game will be remembered as the one that made me popular. That dream did not really come true but it's great that I was honoured in that way.

Interview by **Gary Al-Smith (@garyalsmith)**

Lamptey

RYAN WILLIAMS

Position: AMC

Real-life career: Mansfield Town, Tranmere Rovers, Chesterfield, Hull City, Bristol Rovers, Forest Green Rovers (loan), Aldershot Town (loan), Weymouth, Mansfield Town, Gainsborough Trinity (loan), Gainsborough Trinity

In-game high: Championship Manager 01/02

It was news to Conference North side Gainsborough Trinity that amongst their ranks is an attacking midfield maestro who once compared favourably to Brazilian superstar Kaka.

Assists, goals, pace and (crucially for the discerning gamer) high work rate stats – Ryan Williams of Hull City had it all.

His chief cheerleader, Iain Macintosh, recalls, "Ryan Williams was an absolute miracle worker.

"I actually had to ban myself from buying him. He was so good it felt like cheating.

Williams

"I even snapped him up when I was Manchester United manager in 01/02. He forced his way into the side in no time and became an England regular."

Sadly the real-life version has been living in blissful ignorance of his cyber celebrity status.

Did you really have no idea you led a double life as a world class attacking midfield playmaker?

It's amazing to hear. My mates used to tell me I was pretty good, but I've never had any strange phone calls, presents or stalkers. I feel a bit cheated now.

How did you dodge the diehards for all these years?

No-one's ever mentioned it to me. I'm not much of a computer whiz and I had a kid at a young age – so you can guess how I spent my time! We used to each get a free copy every season and most of the lads in the dressing room were mad on it, so I know how big the game is. My eight-year-old son, Bradley, has just got into it. He loves it, but only ever sticks to managing the big teams. He'll be buzzing when he hears about this and I'll need to check and see if I'm still in the game.

You were at Hull City during the peak of your Champ Man powers. Aside from tearing it up at Trinity, what does the 2012 version of Ryan Williams get up to?

I'm part-time with Gainsborough Trinity and I help out a charity called the SC Foundation, which is enjoyable. Former professional footballers go into schools and try to be role models for the kids. I'll need to tell them all about this.

www.scfoundation.org.uk

STEFAN SELAKOVIC

Position: AMRC

Real-life career: Varbergs GIF, Halmstad, Heerenveen, IFK Goteborg; Sweden (12 caps, 4 goals)

In-game high: Championship Manager 01/02

The best wingers prize vision over velocity, as exemplified by Swedish winger Stefan Selakovic.

A bargain buy from Halmstad at £400,000, his prolific late bursts into the box and set-piece ability more than compensated for a lack of in-game pace.

Tell us about your Championship Manager pedigree, Stefan...

I've played the game every year since 1996, so I guess that makes me an expert!

And how have you put that accumulated knowledge to good use?

I always go Tottenham. They're the team I've supported ever since I was a boy and I've turned them into the best team in the world. Taribo West was a favourite of mine.

Selakovic

He must have been the ultimate Bosman signing. I always signed Mark Kerr and I remember other names like Tonton Zola Moukoko and Cherno Samba. Good times.

What of Stefan Selakovic?

In the earlier versions I always signed myself – when I was good. But I'm getting too old in the game now and I'm only fit for smaller clubs. If I take charge of IFK then it's a different matter. My real life career didn't live up to the one predicted in the game but I've done OK.

Do you still manage to squeeze in a quick game?

Absolutely. The training camps we go on are a dream because it gives me more time to play. My team-mate, Tobias Hysen, is a big fan of the game too and sometimes we manage the same team to see who fares the best. I think every dressing room in football must have players who are keen on Football Manager.

Your friend Anders Svensson told us playing Football Manager sparked off an interest in coaching, now that his playing days on the pitch and in the game are coming to an end. Has it had the same impact on you?

Anders will have to deal with the bench soon enough. He'd better get acquainted with that feeling! I always saw coaching as a natural progression, but I feel like I should qualify for my badges automatically after all these years of playing the game. It's a very good source of knowledge and you pick up different things that I'm sure you could apply to real-life situations. I remember reading with interest that Everton were using the database as part of their scouting setup.

Anything you want us to put to the guys at Sports Interactive?

No, they're doing a good job. Finally after all these years Spurs have a good team with some money to spend. It makes my job a lot easier.

TIM SPARV

Position: DM/AMLC

Real-life career: Southampton, Halmstad, VPS (loan), Groningen; Finland (22 caps)

In-game high: Football Manager 2006

It's worth paying attention to Southampton's esteemed talent factory.

Finnish playmaker Sparv could be snapped up from the Saints for as little as £70,000 and proved equally adept as a defensive midfield shield or a bright spark in the final third.

A real-life stand-out for Groningen and the Finnish national team, his raw talent was perceptively pinpointed by the Sports Interactive scouts.

Of all the players we spoke to for the book, Tim, you were amongst the most excited to be involved. Can we assume you're a fan of the game?

I've been a big fan, right back to when it was called Championship Manager. For the first few years, in particular, I got very addicted and it was like nothing else mattered. I'm sure many people will have thought the same as me, when I'd say to myself 'just one more game'. It was not easy to switch off.

Sparv

Do any of your Champ Man crusades stick in the memory?

I was never interested in managing the big teams with lots of money. I wasn't a glory hunter. I took pleasure in building up small teams from the lower leagues. I found myself going Leyton Orient a lot of the time, despite not knowing anything about them to begin with, and Notts County. And nothing beats signing someone no-one has ever heard of and turning them into a star.

Who were your must-buys?

Not me anyway. I wasn't that good to begin with and it's all about the team, not personal glory – even in a computer game. He wasn't cheap, but I'd always try to get the left-back, Marcelo, from Fluminese. Now he's at Real Madrid in real life. The midfielder Benoit Pedretti was another and I think about him and the game sometimes when I watch French football. There must be a lot of good football knowledge behind Football Manager as most of the players they tip to do well go on to big things.

Including you...

I'm lucky to have had a good career so far. Anything can happen so, who knows, I may end up at Leyton Orient before I finish.

Do your family and friends know about your Football Manager mini-me?

A lot of my friends are addicted to the game too and they are forever threatening to drop me. The nicest thing is that I often get messages from supporters around the world to say that I'm awesome in Football Manager. They'll say things like 'I'll follow you on Twitter because you were so good for my team'. I think it's great that social media allows people to interact like that and that a computer game can bring people together.

TOMMY SVINDAL LARSEN

Position: MLC

Real-life career: Odd Grenland, Start, Odd Grenland (loan), Start, Stabaek, FC Nurnberg, Odd Grenland; Norway (24 caps)

In-game high: Championship Manager 97/98

Tommy Svindal Larsen was the general around which title-winning teams were built.

Snap him up from Staebek and you'd possess a midfield maestro blessed with creativity, passing accuracy and tenacity in the tackle.

TSL carved out a top-flight career in his native land and the Bundesliga with FC Nurnberg, before retiring at 38 years of age in December 2011.

Now he's putting that on-field expertise to good use.

Tommy, how does it feel to have arguably the most famous name in Championship Manager history?

It feels pretty cool! I'm not sure I understand how it all came about but I'm not complaining. No-one's ever really brought it to my attention that I was such a valuable player.

Larsen

Back in the day you were a hot prospect...

One of the scouts must have been very kind to me, but I had some tremendous years when I was young. At 16, I was tipped to be the next big Norwegian player and I was recognised as a greater talent at that point than the likes of Ole Gunnar Solskjaer. But I had some difficult years between 16 and 21. I achieved a lot and had the opportunity to play in Germany and for the national team, even if I didn't quite hit the same heights as Ole.

Ole's a self-confessed Champ Man addict. Have you ever dabbled in it?

I've played the game a few times with my son. He's really into it, as are a few of my friends. I think my family would have turned against me if I got hooked too. However, I do understand the appeal. It's a great learning tool if you want to go on and be a coach or a manager.

With that in mind, what are you up to nowadays?

I've just started a new club – FK Grenland (www. fkgrenland.no). We've gone in at the seventh tier but I've no doubt we'll make it to the top level.

What is the thinking behind that?

Football is in a bad way in Norway just now. The quality isn't that high and the attendance figures are dropping off. Supporters here need football that comes at it from a different angle. We're engaging with the community to use football as a force for good – to help young people who are in trouble at school or those without a job. We're very serious about building this club up.

Are you not tempted to dig your boots out?

My playing days are over but I hope to implement my philosophy on the club. I've always been a great fan of the Barcelona way and people often said I played in their style. That's the approach we want to promote here at FK Grenland, which is a whole new way of thinking. Maybe when we're more established we'll appear in the latest version of Football Manager.

TONTON ZOLA MOUKOKO

Position: AMC

Real-life career: Djurgarden, Derby, Carlstad Utd, IK Sleipner, Syrianska FK, Atlantis FC, IFK Lidingo

In-game high: Championship Manager 00/01

This guy was so good we named a chapter after him.

Deployed behind the strikers, he had no equal – carving the opposition open at will while regularly rattling in 50-plus goal tallies.

Tonton turned down the likes of AC Milan and Juventus to sign for Derby County as a 15-year-old, but off-field problems meant he wasn't able to make the anticipated breakthrough.

In 2003 he re-emerged on trial with Scottish side Falkirk.

Ross Wilson, formerly of Falkirk and currently Watford's head of football business, recalls, "He was a likeable lad, really fit and quick. I've never seen anyone try more step-overs!"

He's currently starring for Swedish minnows IFK Lidingo, the formative club of fellow Championship Manager legend Mikael Dorsin.

You're a hard man to pin down, Tonton...

A lot of people have tried to track me down over the years but it's difficult for them. I don't like Facebook so I'm not on there either. My sister is and she gets a lot of messages from people telling her how well I did for them in the game. Then there are the newspapers.

What about them?

I get newspapers from all over the world, from England to Australia, that want to speak to me. There was a funny example in 2003, when Championship Manager Magazine tried to find me for a story. When they couldn't work out where I was they printed a 'WANTED' poster and offered their readers a $97 cash reward for information on my whereabouts. I laughed at that, especially when my girlfriend and friends joked that I should have told them so they could have got the money!

Does the interest bother you?

It's just harmless fun – if a bit strange. The funny thing is I probably get more people asking me about it now than 10 years ago when I first appeared in the game. It's got so popular now.

When did you first realise that you had such superstar status?

I was a 17-year-old at Derby and I remember going to play in a normal reserve game. But things were different, as a lot of supporters were there and they got excited when they saw me. People started coming to these games looking to talk to me, to get autographs and photos. It was a lot to take in. My agent at the time didn't like it. He would rant about wanting to get in touch with the people who made the game to see about taking me off it. He thought there was too much talk about me.

Has that followed you ever since?

Throughout my career, new team-mates have known who I am because of the game but it's never put me under any additional pressure. We have a laugh about it.

What about the future?

I'm enjoying my football again, which is important, but I still have big hopes for the future. I'm sure something will happen but it's just a case of when. Every day I work hard and hope for the best. I've had offers from lower-league clubs in England but I want to prepare myself properly so I can do myself justice.

Finally, did you play the game?

Yes, of course! When I was at Derby I'd take charge of them. I'd heard so many good things about this 'Tonton Zola Moukoko' guy that I wanted to see for myself. We made a good partnership.

WANTED

CASH REWARD*

TONTON ZOLA MOUKOKO

A reward is waiting for the first person that can tell us where to find him. Photocopy this poster and SUPPORT OUR CAMPAIGN

Sharp-shooting young gun is on the run. Often seen lurking in midfield behind the front two. Is known to be lethal in the world of *CM*. Wanted in Derby, Sweden, Scotland... If you've seen Tonton or know where he is then contact us here:

Wanted! *The Official Championship Manager Magazine*, Future Publishing Ltd, 30 Monmouth Street, Bath BA1 2BW or email cmmag@futurenet.co.uk

*Cash reward of a fistful of dollars, which is $97US, according to our extensive research to be paid to the first person with information leading to a representative of *The Official Championship Manager Magazine* interviewing Tonton. The editor's decision in final.

A FISTFUL OF DOLLARS

This reward is offered to the first hombre (or hombrette) who provides information leading to the interview of Tonton Zola Moukoko, as judged by the editor. The $97US figure was established in a controlled experiment in which a man with average sized hands grasped one dollar bills. He was still able to form a clenched fist while holding 97 bills and none were visible from a side-on, level viewpoint.

THE OFFICIAL CHAMPIONSHIP MANAGER MAGAZINE

WILLIE HOWIE

Position: CM

Real-life career: Partick Thistle, Glenafton, Cumnock Juniors

In-game high: Championship Manager 99/00

The free-scoring Scotsman was part of a Partick Thistle super-team that was tailor-made for bargain-conscious bosses – featuring the likes of Alan Archibald, Alex Martin, Billy MacDonald, John Ritchie, Martin Lauchlan and Robert Dunn.

We hear you're a bit of a Champ Man expert...

I was properly addicted. All my friends were. I still have the odd moment of weakness when I crack and promise myself I'll only play a couple of games, then before I know what's happened three weeks have passed and I'm 15 seasons into a new game.

How did you approach the game?

I'd sign myself for starters, no matter what team I was at. The one thing I never did was cash in. I remember knocking back a £55 million bid from Borussia Dortmund. Thankfully the computer Willie Howie didn't throw the toys out of the pram.

Howie

Any memorable teams or players?

I'd get bored pretty quickly going the bigger teams. The real fun is in lower league challenges. Player-wise, John Welsh at Liverpool was a favourite. Mark Kerr was a no-brainer signing and, if I had a bit of cash, I'd go all-out for Kim Kallstrom and Zlatan Ibrahimovich. The goalkeeper, Andreas Isaksson, was another one. I'd spend hours scouring the Scandinavian market and I still look online for tips.

And the lows?

No matter what I did I could never beat Roma away from home. I must have tried every combination of players and tactics. I remember posting on a messageboard, looking for advice as my favoured 4-3-1-2 with Tonton Zola Moukoko and Youssouf Hersi just wasn't cutting it against them.

Did the in-game fame ever spill over to the real world?

I remember being interviewed by someone from Championship Manager's magazine, who was going all over to speak to the best young players from the game. Sometimes, to this day, I'll be out for a quiet drink and someone will come up and ask if I'm Willie Howie. You prepare yourself for the worst in these situations! Thankfully then they smile and say 'you were great for me in Championship Manager'. At the moment I work for a Sat Nav company, going round the motorways fixing cameras, and I play for Cumnock Juniors. Maybe when this book's out a few folk will come and watch us play.

Playing the game of his life

The inside story of how 'Baby Carrot' went from an obsessive footballing computer geek to the Stamford Bridge hot seat

Andre Villas-Boas
THE NEW SPECIAL ONE

By Duncan White
Sunday Telegraph
Football Correspondent

PREVIOUSLY UNSEEN MATERIAL

Ramaldense team photograph circa 1994 with Villas-Boas circled

His First prizes in football: Ramaldense's trophy 'cabinet'

COLEGIO DE NOSSA SENHORA DO ROSARIO

The motto of Villas-Boas's former club, Marechal Gomes da Costa

you will never drink

The pitch where

Outside his private Ramal home in small block and, un own pit centre, because problem fallow a overgro weeds. Coelho, Benfica Portuga had play them bu Villas-B few of h the club

The block of flats where Villas-Boas met Sir Bobby Robson

PROLOGUE

Andre Villas-Boas is exceptional. By the terms of his profession, he is a prodigy, at 33 becoming the youngest manager to win a European club trophy and doing it in style, with a free-scoring Porto team that caught the covetous eye of a Russian billionaire. Here is a football obsessive whose geeky adolescent fantasies of managing a football club were realised by a chance encounter with Sir Bobby Robson, the manager of Porto, the club he had supported from the moment he knew what a football club was. He started doing his coaching badges before most kids of his age had done their A-Levels and was running the British Virgin Islands national team when most of his school-mates were graduating from university.

Here is a privately-educated son of a professor and a descendant of nobility more than holding his own in the grimy world of football.

The wind from being Robson's protégé to Mourinho's spy and has always pushed those around him to match his resilience: he wants everything fast, including his cars. Chelsea will have to keep up. He doesn't want to grow old as the job planning to use his career to take him round the world: to Japan, Chile and Argentina.

Mourinho once said: "If has taken me 15 years to be an overnight success". Apposite in Villas-Boas's case too. There is little that is ordinary about him except, perhaps, his goalkeeping.

CHAPTER ONE
FAMILY BACKGROUND
Villas-Boas was born in Porto in an upper-middle class

family who neighbourhood [...] Russian [...] lies [...] Filipe, is a [...] had begun [...] before movi [...] his PhD at [...] the Universi [...] Canterbury, [...] classical em [...] the Techno [...] and works [...] makes its co [...] Filipe starre [...] mother, in [...] business, wi [...] clothing sho [...] Villas-[...] affluent family [...] and a brother [...] with the son [...] situated the [...] its Rosaario, one [...] expensive private schools [...] city and with a reputation [...] academic excellence. The school had originally been shown as the English School [...] By Sister Margaret Hutchinson, an Irish nun and other members of the Religious of the Sacred Heart of Mary. He was a polite, affable student but while he was bright he did not study that hard because he was really fascinated him was football," said Joao Eiro, the head of the PE department.

He was obsessed with sport. He was a member of the club

CHAPTER TWO
THE NOBLE ANCESTRY
Villas-Boas's paternal great-grandfather Jose Joaquim Villas-Boas (1835-1906) was the Baron of

CHAPTER THREE
FOOTBALL FANATIC
Villas-Boas was enrolled as a member of FC Porto on July 4, 1980, just before his third birthday. At nine he was part of the family celebrations as they watched Porto beat Bayern Munich in the 1987 European Cup final and he joined a football club called Ribeirense, based in the centre of Porto and the favourite club of the fanatical supporters' groups.

Football consumed him. He started on the 'gateway drugs' football magazines and Panini stickers before slipping down the slope into full-blown Championship Manager addiction. This computer game, with its endless statistics, simulated being a football manager and destroyed the social lives of a generation of football geeks.

Villas-Boas was hooked. He used to carry notebooks around

FANA
Villas-Boas [...] member of FC Porto on July 4, 1980, just before his third birthday. He would become a passionate fan of the club. At nine he was part of the family celebrations as they watched Porto beat Bayern Munich in the 1987 European Cup final and he joined a football club called Ribeirense, based in the centre of Porto and the favourite club of the [...] supporters' groups. [...] Football consumed him. He started on the 'gateway drugs' football magazines and Panini stickers before slipping down the slope into full-blown Championship Manager addiction. This computer game, with its endless statistics, simulated being a football manager and destroyed the social lives of a generation of football geeks.

Villas-Boas was hooked. He used to carry notebooks around

because of financial problems, it lies fallow and is overgrown with weeds. Humberto Coelho, the famous Benfica and Portugal defender, had played for them but when Villas-Boas and a few of his friends joined, the club was struggling.

"I knew were three players I thought were good for the first team, including a small but aggressive defensive midfield player – Villas-Boas," recalls the coach from that period, Quim Espanhol.

"He had been a goalkeeper but he was not that good in goal so was normally on the beach.

"He was a good player, not a big guy but wiry and he had no fear. He talked a lot on the pitch and he always took up good tactical positions. He had to quit at the end of the 1998-99 season though, because he was already working for Porto and had more and more work with them and he could not get his Saturdays free."

CHAPTER FIVE
THE CRUCIAL MEETING
Villas-Boas got his big break in 1994. He was 16 and was living with his parents in what was then a new apartment block on Rua Teixeira Valadim. Sir Bobby Robson and his wife Elsie lived in the same building. As a fanatical Porto fan, Villas-Boas could not help but confront the manager of his club when he bumped into him, wanting to know why he was not playing the striker Domingos Paciencia (who has since gone on to manage Braga and was Villas-Boas's opposite number in the Europa League final). Sir Bobby liked the boy's chutzpah and asked him to have a report on his letterbox. He liked what he read so he asked Villas-Boas to keep writing them for him.

He started to take his protégé down to training. Then he started taking Villas-Boas with him when he went down to first, the area of bars and restaurants at the mouth of the river Douro. Over a meal or coffee, Robson would talk football with his coaching staff and it was there that Villas-Boas first came across Robson's outspoken interpreter, Jose Mourinho.

Robson formalised Villas-Boas's work by telling Porto to take him on as a youth coach but he also helped him to start getting his coaching badges, persuading the Football Association to let him on to a Lilleshall course even though he was still only 17. He even set him up with a placement at his old club Ipswich Town.

"Sir Bobby phoned me and asked if I could have Andre over and let him watch training and show him how the club worked for a few weeks," said George Burley, the manager at the time. "He wanted to know everything. He had listened a lot to Bobby and you could tell he'd had a big influence on him. People compare him to Jose Mourinho and there are things about him that are similar but in terms of his love of very attacking football, well that philosophy came from Bobby. If he can combine the organisation of Mourinho and the inspiration of Bobby then he will be very good indeed."

CHAPTER SIX
A SCOTTISH EDUCATION
Like his siblings and most of his school-friends, Villas-Boas had planned to go to university, and had ambitions of becoming a sports journalist. After meeting Robson, those plans changed. He planned straight into getting his coaching licenses, attending courses at the Largs' Scottish National Sports Centre in Largs.

"Andre first came to us in 1994," said Jim Fleeting, the SFA's director of football development. "He did his C, B, A and Pro Licence with us and was very studious, very dedicated. It must have been daunting coming to a foreign country and being younger than your classmates but he sailed through. I remember he used to read everything he could get his hands on, books on psychology, physiology.

"He did his Pro Licence with a great group: Ally McCoist, Ian Durrant, Owen Coyle. They had a great team spirit. He finished his Pro Licence in 2004 and the following year I asked him to come back and give a presentation to the students. He did a club study and a tactical analysis of an international between Scotland and Georgia. I still use his work as an example to students now."

"At 18 he was not very big but he was a good player for us. He knew he was not good enough to turn professional, though." After leaving Ramaldense he moved to Marechal Gomes de Costa, named after an armchair boulevard in the town, a bit like the Kings Road in London.

"We were all boys from the same social background who loved football," explained Pedro Barros, 39, the club captain. "It has always been quite informal. The team has engineers, doctors and students and it was as coach about the social side as playing." He points to the motto on his club T-shirt: 'You'll never drink alone'.

"Andre joined us in 1998. We had mutual friends and I knew him from playing squash against him at the English club.

CHAPTER SEVEN
CARIBBEAN ADVENTURE
Villas-Boas wanted to put some of his theories into practice and took the first opportunity, becoming technical director of the British Virgin Islands. "We wanted to recruit a young coach with the right qualifications," said Edward Gumrie, who ran the football association.

"He sent us his CV and, coming from a great club like Porto and being a friend of Bobby Robson, we were contacted.

"When he first arrived he was always on the beach, like he was on holiday! But when he started to work he surprised me. He made a plan for all the teams, youth to senior, and had a manual with tactics and training plans, full of information. He was great with computers too.

"He started with the youth team and then wanted to train the seniors. He got some of them coaching the younger players who went on to become internationals so he left a mark."

CHAPTER EIGHT
PORTO AGAIN
When Villas-Boas came back from the Caribbean, things changed quickly. He started working with the Porto youth team again and, in 2002, Mourinho replaced Octavio Machado as manager. He started working for Mourinho on a part-time basis for the end of that season and then took the job full time for 2002-03 season, in which Porto won the league and the Uefa Cup.

He would go undercover to opposition training grounds to judge the mood of the players and assess their fitness before compiling his dossiers and compiling footage on DVDs. Mourinho would call him his "eyes and ears" and took him to Chelsea when he moved there in 2003 and, initially, to Internazionale before Villas-Boas, frustrated at not being given more responsibility, went out alone.

CHAPTER NINE
ACADEMICA
After Villas-Boas stopped working with Mourinho the relationship cooled and he said publicly that they no longer speak. He took a risk joining Academica Coimbra in 2009 because they were threatened with relegation but he got them into mid-table.

The club took a chance, too, of course. "It was a risk, but a calculated risk," said technical director Luis Agostinho. "He was a strong leader who had an excellent training methodology."

Being younger than some of his players, you might have expected him to keep his distance but he forged close bonds with his players. "His age was never a problem," said Pedrinho, who played right-back. "Outside of training he was more like a friend, always wanting to know about your family. He was always first to text you or call you if you got injured. If a player went into hospital for an operation, he would be the first visitor."

When he left for Porto he sent a text message to every player in the squad which read: 'I'm leaving you for a new adventure. I thank you for what we did together. Each one of you has made their mark on me at the start of my career and all in different and special ways.' Villas-Boas is loyal – and is bringing two trusted colleagues with him to Chelsea, Jose Mario Rochis, his fitness trainer, is someone he knows from his time coaching the Porto youth teams while Daniel Sousa drew the job – opposition scout – which he himself used to do for Jose Mourinho.

CHAPTER TEN
FAST LANE
Villas-Boas is a big motorsport fan and in March he was invited by FIA vice-president Carlos Barbosa and the Ford M-Sport team to part-take one of the stages the day before the European round of the World Rally Championship in the Algarve. He sat co-pilot to Matthew Wilson around a 5km test-loop.

Wilson said: "I was massively impressed. He is clearly very intelligent. I have a feeling he is going to turn Chelsea into a force again. He seems to have something about him."

Villas-Boas later attended the Monaco Grand Prix this year and enjoys driving his own cars at speed on the mountain roads of Valongo near Porto. He has driven a BMW Z4 and an M3 and these days drives a special version of the Fiat 500 Abarth.

But Villas-Boas is not flash – and he closely guards the privacy of his family. He no longer gives one-on-one interviews and very rarely appears at public functions with his wife Joana. She studied interior design at Chelsea College of Art and they were married in 2001, but have kept well away from Portugal's lifestyle magazines.

He favec, though, is beginning to impinge on his privacy – the first biography – unauthorised, naturally – is about to be published in Portugal. And these early years chapters is be written yet.

FOOTBALL

Video game is a signing of the times

PREMIERSHIP giant Everton is to use a bestselling computer game to pick promising players.

The club has signed a deal with the makers of Football Manager to get an early look at its database of 370,000 players worldwide.

The footballers are researched and rated by Football Manager's huge team of scouts across the world so its players can pick dream sides.

Among the stars that Football Manager has picked out in the past are Wayne Rooney and Argentinian wizard Lionel Messi.

Football Manager's Miles Jacobson said: "This formal recognition by a Premier League team is fantastic."

Click off . . boss Moyes

Everton's vid game manager

By GUY PATRICK

EVERTON FC have signed a ground-breaking deal to use a soccer management computer game to scout for new players.

Manager David Moyes and his coaches will link up with bestselling simulator Football Manager, which uses 1,000 scouts to compile its huge database.

They will be able to track more than 370,000 players and staff from 20,000 teams worldwide.

Football Manager creators, brothers Paul and Oliver Collyer, have been flooded with offers from clubs since developing the first version of the game in 1992. Their firm Sports Interactive accepted Everton's offer as the brothers are both Toffees fans.

Paul said: "The game's database is the most extensive scouting network in football.

"This is as close to my boyhood dream of playing at Goodison Park as I will ever get."

ALAN FETTIS

Position: GK

Real-life career: Glentoran, Ards, Hull City, West Brom (loan), Nottingham Forest, Blackburn Rovers, Leicester City (loan), York City, Hull City, Sheffield Utd (loan), Grimsby Town (loan), Macclesfield Town, Bury; Northern Ireland (25 caps)

In-game high: Championship Manager 96-97

I know all about Championship Manager! Back in my playing days I got a free copy and I know from playing it briefly how addictive it was. My brother-in-law was right into it and would keep me up to date on my progress in the game. Nowadays I'm the goalkeeping coach for Manchester United's academy teams and I know it's still popular within the dressing room.

BILLY JONES

Position: D/DM/MRLC

Real-life career: Crewe, Preston, West Brom

In-game high: Football Manager 2005

Random supporters would tell me I was doing a great job for them in the game. They must look at me on the pitch now and wonder what happened! I got hooked on it one summer and I tend to go the bigger teams with money to spend. I only ever last a couple of months before I'm sacked, though. I take too much enjoyment from dumping the prima donnas in the reserves and fining them, which never goes down well.

DANIEL BRAATEN

Position: FLC

Real-life career: Skeid, Rosenborg, Bolton, Toulouse; Norway (34 caps, 2 goals)

In-game high: Championship Manager 03/04

Everyone in football knows all about Championship/ Football Manager. No matter what club you're at or which country you're in, you can bet there will be a group of players in every dressing room who are addicted to it. I steered clear, but friends told me I was good in the 2003/04 version. I think the scouts got my pace statistics right, but I'm sorry I couldn't score as many in real life as I could in the game! It's flattering to think that, in a few years' time, people who have never seen me play will remember a cheap attacker from Skeid who was value for money.

DEAN KEATES

Position: DM

Real-life career: Walsall, Hull City, Kidderminster Harriers, Lincoln City, Walsall, Peterborough Utd, Wycombe Wanders, Wrexham

In-game high: Championship Manager 99/00

About ten years ago I travelled to Glasgow with Walsall for a pre-season tour. This little kid, who couldn't have been more than seven years old, ambled up asking which one of us was Dean Keates. When I put my hand up he said 'You're the best player in Championship Manager. I've got you in my team – you're unbelievable'. It makes more sense after hearing about this book.

RENE MIHELIC

Position: AMLC

Real-life career: Maribor, Nacional; Slovenia (3 caps)

In-game high: Football Manager 2008

I play the game, as do a lot of my friends and team-mates. But I had no idea I was highly rated within the game. That comes as a big surprise, albeit a welcome one. It's a nice thought to think that so many people know me from Football Manager. When I have a go I like to play as AS Roma because Francesco Totti has always been my idol.

SERGE MAKOFO

Position: DR

Real-life career: MK Dons, Kettering Town, Maidenhead Utd, Halesowen Town, Potters Bar Town, Croydon Athletic, Grays Athletic, Burton Albion (loan), Kettering Town, Grimsby Town

In-game high: Championship Manager 4

I used to get letters about this when I was at MK Dons. Even now I get the odd one through. They'll talk about me being cheap to buy, scoring a lot of goals and then moving on to someone like Real Madrid. I looked it up on the Internet and only recently found out what 'CM' meant. It all makes a bit more sense now!

BACKPACK TO THE FUTURE

Gap year? Mid-life crisis? Then why not take some time to finally see the players that you have built your teams around for the past 20 years?

If you're very nice, perhaps these legendary figures will even pose for a picture with you after the game and sign a match programme - or your copy of Football Manager Saved My Life. If you do manage to track any of them down, send all relevant documentation to backpage@ backpagepress.co.uk and earn your place in our FM Stalkers Hall of Fame.

But be quick! These guys tend to move around a lot!

#1 SWITZERLAND
Alexander Farnerud – playing for Young Boys, Berne
Joao Paiva – playing for Grasshoppers Zurich

#2 SWEDEN
Anders Svensson – playing for Elfsborg
Stefan Selakovic – playing for IFK Goteborg
Tonton Zola Moukoko – playing for IFK Lidingo, island off Stockholm

#3 NORWAY
Cherno Samba – playing for FK Tonsberg
Tommy Svindal Larsen – coach, FK Grenland

#4 ENGLAND
Gareth Jelleyman – playing for Boston Utd
John Welsh – playing for Preston North End
Serge Makofo – playing for Grimsby Town
Michael Duff – playing for Burnley
Michael Dunwell – playing for Billingham Town
Ryan Williams – playing for Gainsborough Trinity

#5 SPAIN
Kennedy Bakircioglu – playing for Racing Santander

#6 SCOTLAND
Mark Kerr – playing for Dunfermline
Willie Howie – playing for Cumnock Juniors

#7 HOLLAND
Tim Sparv – playing for Groningen

#8 WALES
Dean Keates – playing for Wrexham

#9 FRANCE
Daniel Braaten – playing for Toulouse

#10 PORTUGAL
Rene Mihelic – playing for Nacional

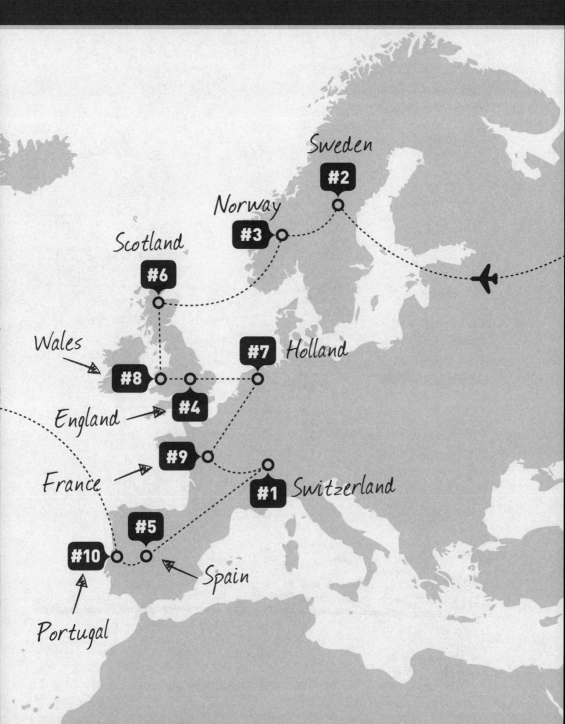

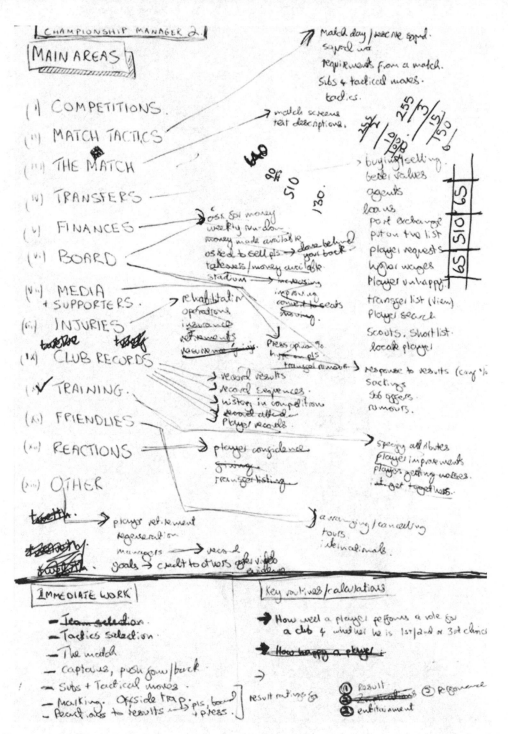

/ The masterplan for CM2 – organised chaos.

FOOTBALL MANAGER STOLE MY LIFE

Broken homes, broken bones
and broken phones

When we went looking for stories of how this game had crossed over into the lives of those who play it, we had no idea what to expect, but car crashes, police raids, and straight-up stalking wouldn't have been on the list. How wrong we were.

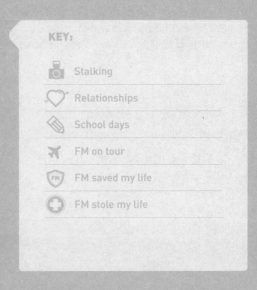

KEY:

📷 Stalking

♡ Relationships

✏ School days

✈ FM on tour

🛡 FM saved my life

✚ FM stole my life

LOST IN TRANSLATION

ARTA WILDEBOER

In 2006, I attended a semester abroad in Seville during my final year of college, armed with my laptop and a copy of Football Manager.

In honour of my new home for the semester, I chose to start a season with Sevilla FC. Fond memories of Dani Alves and Fredi Kanoute still flood my mind now as I type.

Being the gregarious type, I spoke incessantly about Spanish football with the directors of my program any time I was afforded the chance. They all were very impressed by my knowledge of Spanish football, which I had gained from so many hours watching my little dots fly around the screen.

> To prepare for the interview, I switched the language setting on FM to Spanish

Deep down I felt like I was cheating a little, since most of my familiarity came from those precious hours ignoring my girlfriend and school work in front of the laptop, instead of watching actual games, which were so hard to find on US television.

One day while at school, I was approached by Mario, one of the directors of my program, who asked me if I had a job while in Seville. I scoffed, since I was there to drink beer and chase women and ostensibly to learn a bit of Spanish, which at the time I did not speak at all. He asked me if I was amenable to the idea of working unpaid, to which I replied 'yes', albeit suspiciously.

The job, as it turned out, was to change my life.

Apparently, impressed with my knowledge of Spanish football, which he was blissfully unaware I had gleaned solely from hours upon hours of scouting teams and playing matches on FM, he told me that Sevilla FC had a position open in the marketing department for a Spanish to English translator.

Seville is a city with a smalltown vibe, where everybody knows everyone else in their particular section of the city, and Mario's parents' neighbour's son was the assistant to the director of marketing at Sevilla FC.

I stood there in a bit of shook for a moment. I gathered myself and replied that I would be extremely interested, knowing full well that my knowledge of Spanish was limited to the words 'Ole' and 'Gol' and hiding that precious fact from Mario. He then told me he would get back to me and soon I had a call from him telling me to meet him at a coffeeshop near the stadium to meet Curro, the neighbour's son.

To prepare for my interview, I switched the language setting on FM to Spanish and did my best to write down notes on Spanish translations for each position on the pitch, football-related idioms and the like.

I committed to memory every team member's statistics, past clubs, and other tidbits that FM could provide about Sevilla FC, and their youth team ranks as well.

As fate would have it, Curro was more interested on the occasion of my interview to practise his English, to my great relief. The interview consisted of me spilling my guts on my love affair with Dani Alves, though I failed to mention my love was directed to the little round dot version of my hero, who marauded down the right side of the electronic green pitch of my laptop screen.

Arta Wildeboer

I was told that I could start the next week, and that the marketing offices were inside of the stadium. On my first day I felt as if I was in a surreal fantasy. I was given an ID card and was now privy to a very special place during a very special year for the team. Given full access to the stadium, I explored every inch, though I was barred, along with everyone else, from actually walking on that beautiful pitch.

I couldn't help but be nervous that they would soon find out that I didn't speak a lick of Spanish, and was hardly up to the task of translating the first half-season's match reports. I begged and cajoled my classmates and even my girlfriend back at school in Arizona to help me with the translation.

After the first day I was contemplating how I would break the news to my boss that I was not up to the job due to my lack of Spanish, but this was the team's 100th anniversary year, when Sevilla won their first of two Uefa Cups and the luck rubbed off on me, in conjunction with a bit of hard work. My boss insisted on speaking English in the office in order better to learn, so I was able to take the first two weeks or so to learn enough Spanish to do a quickie translation that no one at the club could read anyway.

Satisfied that my position was safe, I settled into the next few months of watching games while proudly displaying my club ID card to whoever tried to stop me sitting where I pleased, and explaining in broken Spanish that I was the official club translator, which in retrospect sounds absurd.

On my first day at work I attended the press conference marking the signing of Julien Escude from Ajax. After my first match working for the team, I was taken in by my boss to the press conference, where I was able sit in the front row and draw a bemused stare from Juande Ramos as he saw me furiously snapping away with my camera.

Handshakes with Saviola in his final season with the club and pictures of Fredi Kanoute from two feet away, who I freaked out when I yelled "good game, Fredi" in English, which I suppose he was not expecting to hear in Southern Spain, remain strong in my memory.

I was introduced to the club's youth director, who looked at me wide-eyed while I rattled off names of youth team members like Lolo and the now departed Antonio Puerta, who was just breaking into the first team at the time. I marvelled at how short Jose Maria del Nido, the chairman, was - and for an alleged mob attorney, he was a very nice man.

Dozens of such experiences followed and the season was a special one for not only me, but the club and I honestly owe it all to Football Manager.

Although I never did get to meet Dani Alves, who was partly responsible for me getting the job, I did walk off with one of his jerseys as a parting gift from the club.

Vamos mi Sevilla, Vamos Campeon!

Kanoute

FALSE NUMBER 999

ADAM CLERY

There was no greater example of my commitment to FM than when my parents were away and I got my Hibernian side to the Uefa Cup final.

While I was hooking my laptop up to the TV downstairs, I thought, 'You should wear your suit for this. If it was a real game you'd wear a suit'. So I did.

The game was end to end stuff; an enthralling cup classic. Towards the end of the first half there was a coming together, the referee played on and Wolfsburg scored. This just completely flipped my lid. It looked like one of the dots had really lunged in: a clear foul. I'm still angry.

I got the lads in at half time and I gave myself five minutes to lay into them. In terms of detail or emotion, nothing was held back.

The second half was everything the first half had been, and more. We hit the post, shots were cleared off the line, we had a penalty shout. I was going through the whole range of emotions. The pressure was starting to tell and there was a foul on the edge of the box.

We got a penalty. I paused the game and went all Alan Pardew, but instead of there being another manager there, there was nobody; nobody except a metaphorical rest-of-the-world. I composed myself, pressed resume and Andy Carroll slotted home the spot kick. The tide had turned. Their resolve was broken, their spirit shattered.

The tension was building when there was a bang on the front door. It was like a horror film where the victim was hiding in a barn with some sort of wild ox trying to charge it down. Reality set in. I was startled so much I just didn't answer it. Another knock, louder. I pressed pause and I crept towards the door.

As the door creaked open, a blue light flooded in. I could make out the nervous outline of my frail neighbour, flanked by two policemen. Knowing that I was alone in the house and having heard all these screams and shouts for over an hour, he thought he'd better call the local constabulary to check I was ok.

The officers asked me what was going on. I was going to say I was having a fight with my girlfriend, but I'm glad I didn't. I think my life would have turned out differently had I gone down that route. I swallowed my pride and explained I was playing a game. The more senior copper gave me a lecture, but I swear the other one was a player. He looked at me and in one glance said, "I know, mate".

23-07-2011 23:35 #1

LA FURIA ROJA:
FC Oss Researcher

MEMBER
#174408 (Formerly Aussieant32)

JOIN DATE:
11th November 2008

POSTS
3,452

LOCATION
Terrassa, Spain - FC Barcelona

I have fallen in love with my FM Club so much that I am flying abroad to watch them!

Sorry, i know this isn't really about the game itself but I wanted to share. I have really only played one save on FM this year, FC Oss. For those that don't know they are in the Dutch 3rd tier and doing Gundo's challenge they got promoted to the Erste Division. Now my best mate, in Wales, also did the challenge and got the same team and we both fell in love with the club. We made a deal, if they ever won promotion IRL to the Erste we would go watch them, well that happened and on the 14th of October we are both flying to Amsterdam then getting a train to Oss to watch them against Veenam.

I contacted the club and they want to run up a little story on their website about us coming over and thankfully are being really helpful with regards to getting us tickets etc.

Anyway, apologies again for posting a non PC related thread but most of us are active here and I wanted to share

Thanks all.

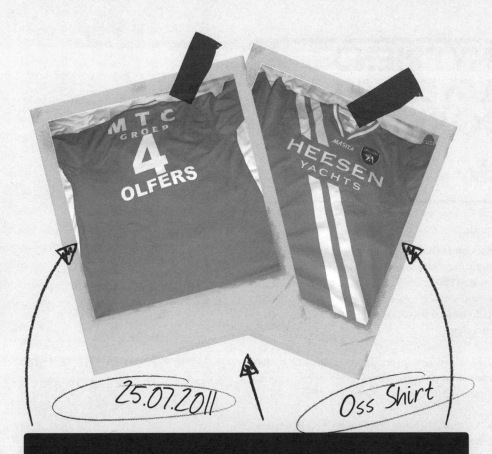

25.07.2011

Oss Shirt

25-07-2011 23:46

LA FURIA ROJA:
FC Oss Researcher

MEMBER
#174408 (Formerly Aussieant32)

JOIN DATE:
11th November 2008

POSTS
3,453

LOCATION
Terrassa, Spain - FC Barcelona

We also both signed a player, Steve Olfers, neither of us mentioned it to each other, it was just coincidence, anyway he sort of became a legend between the two of us so we both are getting Oss shirts with Olfers on the back!

MY FRIEND LOVES YOU, MARK KERR

GRANT SALES

Back on FM2005, I loved a player by the name of Mark Kerr. A tenacious, scrappy midfielder with Dundee United who, according to the game, would be one of the greats. I bought him for every save I had, and ordered his shirt from the Dundee United club shop.

Over Christmas, a friend mentioned that her boyfriend had tickets to the Dundee United players' dinner and that Mr Kerr would be there.

After much begging, recounting of FM stories and offering of favours, she promised to get me his autograph. So, fast-forward to the night in question, and she is sitting on a table waiting for the right opportunity. After an hour, he got up and started to head towards the door. My friend saw her chance. She barrelled after him as he passed through a door ... and straight into the toilets.

They both stood looking at each other until she blurted out: "My friend loves you!"

His face grew even more confused.

She tried again. "On Football Manager. He says you're a legend."

Another blank look.

"Can he have your autograph?"

Normality resumed and he signed a dinner programme for me.

That and my shirt are in storage now, but it's something I'll bring up if I ever get to meet him myself.

> After an hour, he got up and headed for the door; my friend saw her chance

NO SUBSTITUTE FOR SLEEP

CHRIS McINTYRE

Back when I was 15, Championship Manager was my life. It was the craze in school.

Everyone talked about it – who to sign, where we were in the league tables, boasting about cup victories and ganging up on the cheats who took charge of two teams to get players for free.

Every spare minute was spent playing Champ Man – from the moment I got in from school until my alarm went off in the morning. I wasn't sleeping throughout the week so I could play that extra game, win another trophy, finish another season and secure that one last signing. Unless I was physically kicked out the front door, there was no way I'd have left my computer screen. Then at weekends I could devote two full days to gaming.

I remember my eyes were constantly heavy, but removing myself from the game wasn't an option.

Looking back now at photos, each day I looked rougher and rougher. But the bags under my eyes could have been 10kg kettlebells – I wasn't giving into sleep.

I lasted 11 straight days before crashing out on my school desk. I was sent straight to the guidance teacher, who started asking if I had problems at home. It was at that point that I burst out laughing and told him about the game. When I got home it had disappeared from my computer. I was in floods of tears, distraught after all the hard work I'd put in to achieve the dream team.

I got a massive row from my mum and was sent to bed. I was so exhausted that I crashed out instantaneously and slept through the next day - missing another day of school in the process.

After that, I knew I couldn't keep doing that myself and that it was impacting on every area of my life.

So I just played it at a friend's house instead. I felt I was back in control but how wrong I was. I didn't come home, we stayed up all night and my friend ended up getting hooked. That ended with a month's grounding and hefty punishments.

Thankfully I then discovered women and my life has changed for the better. But I still pine for a bit of Champ Man action.

The guidance teacher asked if I had problems at home. I burst out laughing and told him about the game

GOD SAVE THE QUINIELA

JUAN C RIAL

It was about 2004. I was unemployed and, even though I lived with my parents, only €150 remained in my bank account, so I almost couldn't afford to pay my bills (internet, mobile, partying at weekends).

I was a long-time gambler on the famous Quiniela in Spain (like the football pools in the UK) and I had the idea to generate a whole season of results in Football Manager and use them to bet on the fixtures for that weekend.

The Saturday games were all okay, I hit four or five matches. At 6.30pm I turned the radio on to listen to the end of the Liga matches and I realised that I was hitting all eight games!

Then in injury time the referee whistled a penalty for Mallorca. Samuel Eto'o - he was still playing in the Islands - missed!

I looked at my ticket and saw that I had hit 13 games.

So there was only one game left: Valencia vs Real Sociedad.

I bet for a home win or an away win. The only result that was not good for me was a draw.

Then I turned the TV on and started to watch it. In the second half, Sociedad scored twice, but in the last 20 minutes Valencia managed to draw - the luck I had with Eto'o was lost in this game.

I won about €7000, so I could keep partying for a long time, but I always think that if the last result had been different, the prize would have been around €60,000. It could had changed my life.

FM BROKE MY FOOT

SIMON FURNIVALL

I've been playing the game since CM97/98 and in that time I've broken toes on four separate occasions. I have a habit of kicking things when I'm angry and during my angst-ridden teenage years that meant kicking things very hard indeed.

The worst occasion was back on CM01/02 when, having taken Scunthorpe from the third tier to the Premier League, a season-long battle against relegation ended with a final day game against Leicester. We needed a point to stay up but were losing 1-0 and missed a late penalty. I took it very badly, booted my desk and broke two of my toes.

I went with the 'tell the doctor and family as little as possible' approach and would only let on that I'd kicked my desk because I was angry, not why I was angry. My family were already irritated by how much I played the game. If they knew it had caused physical injury I suspect that would have been the last time I played it. My friends, however, laughed themselves silly. Only one of them played the game, and he was a little more understanding, but any time I was ill or injured for the next few years jokes were inevitably made about it being CM-related.

THE INTERVENTION

MATT McMAHON

Going off to university is an exciting time for most people, but despite all the wonders of being away from home with the world seemingly at my feet, I still craved the Champ Man hit and I didn't have a computer of my own to play it on. The first few weeks were fine and dandy - I joined the football team, made new friends and got very drunk on lots of occasions. But still something was missing.

I had an essay to finish and was moaning about having to go all the way into university to write it up when my mate suggested I could borrow his laptop. Whilst typing, I wanted a quick Champ Man break. Just a few hours or so to help 'refocus the mind'. Suddenly it dawned on me that I could make a regular habit of 'borrowing' my mate's laptop to 'write essays'. I phoned home and asked them to post the Champ Man disc to me so I could realise this wonderful dream.

> I phoned home and asked them to post the Champ Man disc to me

I didn't sleep well that night, excited at the thought of getting back into the Champ Man groove. I contemplated what team to manage, who to sign and what formation to play. It was going to be epic.

I had to wait for a few days for the disc to arrive. When I got my hands on the laptop, I played and played for all I was worth, we were like an adulterous couple spending every possible minute together, staying up late, making the most of our time together. On Champ Man days, when I had access to the laptop, I would annoy friends with my non-attendance at social gatherings. By that I mean trips to the pub.

I did become aware that Champ Man was taking up a lot my time, but it always had, so I thought nothing of it. But university opened my eyes to many new things. Some people didn't like football. Some people didn't even like sports. Some had never even heard of Champ Man. This I had not bargained for – the lack of understanding from non-players was hard to take. There were comments made about me 'playing Champ Man again', threats about deleting my game. I wrote it off as banter.

> I could see 'Are you sure you want to delete Forza Inter?' I could see him click 'Yes' and not 'Cancel'

When there was a knock at my door one evening, my initial displeasure at the Champ Man interruption turned to blind panic. In a scene copied from the popular Channel 5 programme Rough American Cops Arrest and Pin Down Suspects in an Over-Aggressive Manner Causing Serious Harm to the Suspect, I was held kicking and fighting by three men while one took control of my (his) laptop, accessed my game and pressed delete. He made sure I could see him do it, too. I could see 'Are you sure you want to delete 'Forza Inter?'. I could see him click 'Yes' and not 'Cancel'.

Like a bullied schoolboy who knows his atomic wedgie is not getting any worse, I just sat there dumbfounded. How could they?

RELEASE CLAUSE

KIERAN MCKENNA

A few of the lads at our school were obsessed with FM. We'd sit in little groups in our classes and talk tactics, as well as the little gems we'd uncover and the great results we had.

One day we were sat in history class, scribbling down tactics in the back of our books when the teacher asked us what we were doing. When we couldn't give a proper answer we were obviously in a bit of bother. I was told then that I wouldn't be allowed to take history as a GCSE, and I would have to take Business Studies instead.

I guess you could say it worked out. I took Business at A level, and then at university level and am working towards a degree.

And, of course, I still play FM.

We were sat in history class, scribbling down tactics in the back of our books when the teacher asked us what we were doing

26-07-2011 23:29 #41

LA FURIA ROJA:
FC Oss Researcher

MEMBER
#174408 (Formerly Aussieant32)

JOIN DATE:
11th November 2008

POSTS
3,454

LOCATION
Terrassa, Spain - FC Barcelona

Originally Posted by Random-86

*Some nice trivia you might like to know about them.
FC Oss was previously known as TOP Oss, which was
a little over a year ago now. You also mentioned they will
be playing against Veendam. They are currently known as
SC Veendam, but only a couple of months ago they were
known as BV Veendam. Maybe you can impress some
people with the not so obvious knowledge. FC Oss was
the first team ever to relegate from the second division
and, now, also the first team ever to be promoted to that
division. Have fun in Oss.*

> *Cheers mate, i have actually sunk myself into the
> dutch system since taking over, I just fell in love
> with it. Barca will always be my team, not only cause
> of my passion for them but also as they are pretty
> deeply steeped into my family history, but I dont see
> the problem with having a 2nd team to love!*
>
> *On a side note, I have actually started my Oss save
> again, I got to the 2040's but it just got too easy, I won
> the league last year by 14 points and the following
> I started with Ajax away, Twente home and PSV away,
> I won all 3 with a f/a of 16/0! So I am back to the erste
> and battling for every point*

31.07.2011

31-07-2011 07:22 #51

LA FURIA ROJA:
FC Oss Researcher

MEMBER
#174408 (Formerly Aussieant32)

JOIN DATE:
11th November 2008

POSTS
3,455

LOCATION
Terrassa, Spain - FC Barcelona

We booked out accommodation this morning :P

just counting the days now, its going to be immense! Cant wait to pull on my first FC Oss shirt after all these years.

OUT FOR THE SEASON

HAKON POR PALSSON

In 1998 I was 13 years old and I broke both my ankles and tore every sinew and ligament inside them playing football. It took me nine months to recover. On top of that my parents just got divorced and it was ugly, it tore my family apart. I couldn't walk, I wasn't fit enough to go to school, I was alone for most of my days.

A family friend knew of my football enthusiasm and gave me Championship Manager 98. I finished 24 seasons in those nine months, leading Wolverhampton Wanderers to unimaginable glories. Twelve Premier Division victories, eight Champions League victories and so many Carling and FA Cups I don't remember.

Championship Manager got me through my injuries and was more or less my only companion. It gave me a reason to get out of bed.

Finally my injuries subsided, though the repercussions still haunt me today (my Injury Proneness must be at least 17).

Today a grown man with a family, a house and a dog, I still play, especially during the last five months - I got injured again and had little to do but physiotherapy and be with my family and my old friend, my grand companion, Football Manager.

I would like to thank the Collyer brothers, and hope that eventually they get to read this story, for this never-ending, nerve-wracking, brilliant game they made. I probably owe them my sanity. Thanks Paul and Ov.

> Championship Manager got me through my injuries and was more or less my only companion. It gave me a reason to get out of bed.

FOR THE LOVE OF THE GAME

MARK COOPER

I've been playing Championship/Football Manager since the first game back in 1993. i had to play at my friend's house, until I eventually bugged my father into stumping up for a PC in 1995. Neither I nor my friend had girlfriends at the time, which was probably a good thing.

Four years later I decided to move to America with friends who had lived in England. My best friend bought me a copy of Championship Manager 99/00 as a going away present. I played it for months and months. I then started going out with a friend of a friend, and she knew I was right into the game. We got married in September 2001 and then all of a sudden the game just vanished. No explanation – it was just gone.

More than a bit confused, I didn't play the game for three years, as it wasn't so easy to get hold of in America back then and the shipping would have cost too much to import it in. I got a lucky break when SEGA joined up with Sports Interactive and made it available as a digital download. I later bought the CD version, too. So I played the game again for a while, though it upset my wife. At the time I had no idea why, but she said she couldn't understand why I enjoyed something with no flashy graphics that was basically just a list of stats.

We decided to move back to Europe in 2007 and, amazingly, my copy disappeared again. I knew exactly where I packed it and was pretty upset, so my wife accused me of loving the game more than her. Despite living in Ireland, where it was much easier to get hold of the game, I didn't play it.

My wife walked out on me in August 2007, taking my children back with me to America. It wasn't all bad. I no longer needed to rent the size of house I was in, and my landlord was happy because he was looking to sell the property anyway. So he let me stay there rent-free for two months. With the money I saved I bought a nice laptop and a brand new copy of Football Manager 2007 – two days after my wife left.

I played non-stop for two weeks, then got my stuff together and moved back to America. For a few months I lived with my friends, going through divorce proceedings and playing the game.

I started dating someone from my old work. We moved in together and I started playing FM on her computer. We had money problems, so I'd sold my laptop.

> My wife accused me of loving the game more than her.

Then one day my copy of the game disappeared into thin air – the third time it had happened. A friend told me my girlfriend hated me playing it as it stopped her playing Farmville on Facebook. Needless to say we didn't last long, and I moved closer to my children in late 2009.

I started seeing a woman I worked with, who is not into video games at all, but she likes to watch me play Football Manager. I'd tell her all my funny stories from the game.

She's now my fiancée and bought me a copy of FM 2011 for my 38th birthday. She's never once complained about my playing it.

So, in closing, if your wife or girlfriend harasses you about playing Football Manager, you can always find someone else that will accept your addiction.

Eventually.

Divorce!

BY 'MIKE ASHLEY'S PANIC BUTTON'
Taken from Football Ramble forum

A mate of mine was sixth in the Championship with one game to go, and needed just a point against an already-promoted Middlesbrough to clinch a play-off place. He raced into a 2-0 lead only to see Dave Kitson score in the 60th minute. Kitson then popped up with a 90th-minute equaliser, which meant my mate finished seventh and had another season of Championship football to put up with. But the best part of the story is still to come.

The weekend arrived and our team, Peterborough United, happened to be playing Middlesbrough. We took our usual position at the front of the London Road terrace and anticipated a heavy defeat. Who scored two goals? Dave Kitson.

After the second goal he celebrated right in front of us. The look on my mate's face was absolutely priceless.

To this day, whenever Kitson's name is mentioned my friend's face turns a crimson colour.

> My girlfriend hated me playing it as it stopped her playing Farmville on Facebook.

GRAHAM ALEXANDER, INTERRUPTED

ADAM MORRIS

I genuinely feel that if I'm mid-game and my girlfriend comes in, it has a negative impact on the team. It really does seem that her entrance into a room gives the opposition a lift. I sometimes call her their 12th man. I've got proof.

Some years ago, while in charge at Partick Thistle, I had reached the Scottish Cup quarter-finals. My league form was drab, but I'd somehow managed to take Rangers to a penalty shoot-out at Firhill after a 0-0 draw.

Kellie was at her friend's house, so I had absolute concentration on the task in hand. The lights were low, Air's Moon Safari was on in the background, and I had a glass of red wine to enjoy the occasion with.

What a start to the shoot-out: my team scored twice (Liam Buchanan and Paul McManus) and Rangers missed both (Steven Davis and Toto Tamuz). Score the third and it's in the bag, I thought, and the taker was Graham Alexander, whom I'd signed on a free in the summer. I'd picked him third on purpose, thinking it would be a crucial pen.

The ball was placed, he stood hands on hips at the edge of the area... the keeper wouldn't have a chance with this. And then - BUZZ! Kellie had forgotten her keys and was full of beans, dying to tell me about her day at work and her evening. I even had to fetch her a glass of wine.

The lights went on full beam, off went 'La Femme d'Argent' and on blared America's Next Top Model. I regained my composure and hit the space bar to continue the shoot-out. Kellie was still talking, but I'd blocked her out. Up stepped Alexander – who hit it straight at his namesake Neil in the Rangers goal. I missed all my remaining spot kicks. They scored all of theirs. I slumped heartbroken in front of the PC, while Kellie - unaware of the ruin she had precipitated - smiled innocently as Tyra Banks sent another budding model home.

Five days later, as we sat in a pub, she said: "You've been off with me for a few days. What is it?"

> I'd picked him third on purpose, thinking it would be a crucial pen

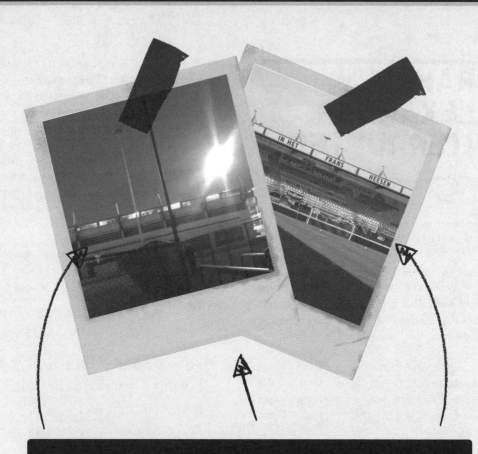

13-10-2011 09:54 #62

LA FURIA ROJA:
FC Oss Researcher

MEMBER
#174408 (Formerly Aussieant32)

JOIN DATE:
11th November 2008

POSTS
3,452

LOCATION
Terrassa, Spain - FC Barcelona

Hi again all.

Just letting you know that the game is tomorrow. We fly out at 7 am. Club have confirmed that our custom shirts and match tickets are in the club shop waiting for us. Cant wait, will get some photos etc up.

POST #75 – PART 1

LA FURIA ROJA:
FC Oss Researcher

MEMBER
#174408 (Formerly Aussieant32)

JOIN DATE:
11th November 2008

POSTS
3,452

LOCATION
Terrassa, Spain - FC Barcelona

Well we are back, and what a trip!!

We started off heading straight for Centraal Station after checking into our hotel with the intention of just grabbing our tickets to Oss and then heading in a bit later as it was only 11am and kick off wasn't until 8pm. We managed to survive one hour before we jumped on the train, we just couldn't wait.

We didn't think to get directions etc to the ground so we just thought to wing it, this wasn't a great idea as it took us 2 hours to do a 20 minute journey, but when we walked around the corner and saw the Frans Heensen Stadium in front of us, all frustrations were forgotten, I turned to my mate and simply said "We are here".

We went to the club shop and got our shirts and I got a scarf and a key ring. We asked Sylvia, the lovely lady who made most of this possible, where the supporters sit. She advised us that the 'tough' group sit in the C stand so we had 2 tickets for that!

POST #75 – PART 2

LA FURIA ROJA:
FC Oss Researcher

MEMBER
#174408 (Formerly Aussieant32)

JOIN DATE:
11th November 2008

POSTS
3,452

LOCATION
Terrassa, Spain - FC Barcelona

Now, really there is nothing to do at or around the stadium 4 hours before kick off so we headed back into the town centre for a pub. We walked into a pub called "'T Libre". Not 20 seconds from sitting down one of the 3 men at the bar calls over to us,

"You are at the wrong pub for Top Oss (the old name of the team), the supporters drink a bit further down the road. We got chatting and explained that we had never been and had travelled from Australia and the UK. They could not believe it, the chap we were speaking to, Djippie (pronounced Jippee) even tried calling the local media to get them to take our story, he wasn't able to get anyone to come out which was a shame. Djippie explained that he was a regular at the game and offered to go to the match with us and introduce us to everyone, we gladly accepted.

POST #75 – PART 3

LA FURIA ROJA:
FC Oss Researcher

MEMBER
#174408 (Formerly Aussieant32)

JOIN DATE:
11th November 2008

POSTS
3,452

LOCATION
Terrassa, Spain - FC Barcelona

When we got to the game it was pretty clear he wasn't exaggerating, he was stopped every 10 seconds by someone saying hello! We went into the Oss pub inside the ground and then at kick off up to the stand. It was incredible how we were treated, everyone was so nice to us, welcoming us and making sure we were included in all the chants etc. 2 very kind people even gave us their own scarves from the Oss won promotion last season, we were told that these were no longer available so were very touched by this gesture.

Now to the game itself, what a game it was!

It started well, Oss took and early lead through De Ruiter on the 7th minute. Veendam equalised on the 24th but Oss soon took the lead again through Bieber on the 28th. We were all over them until Arends miss hit his goal kick and trying to recover took the striker down, and although he wasn't the last line he received a straight red on the 35th. 2 goals in 2 minutes from Veendam put us 3-2 down at the break.

POST #75 – PART 4

LA FURIA ROJA:
FC Oss Researcher

MEMBER
#174408 (Formerly Aussieant32)

JOIN DATE:
11th November 2008

POSTS
3,452

LOCATION
Terrassa, Spain - FC Barcelona

The boys came back out but Veendam were just knocking it around and looking to hold the lead, in the 56th they were awarded a very soft penalty and at 4-2 and a man down Oss looked like they were done for.

That was until Marcel Van Der Sloot took control of a loose pass 35 yards out in the 63rd minute, skinned his opponent and bent one in off the bar from 25 right in front of the Oss faithful to send us into raptures! 4-3 and Oss were flying. We were all over them and in the 76th when we won a corner it could only have one ending, Bart Van Muyen nodded it home and Oss were level and the stand was shaking!!

We attacked for the rest of the match but it ended 4-4, what a way to end a fantastic experience.

Needless to say, we WILL be back to Oss.
Few pictures below.

POST #75 – PART 5

LA FURIA ROJA:
FC Oss Researcher

MEMBER
#174408 (Formerly Aussieant32)

JOIN DATE:
11th November 2008

POSTS
3,452

LOCATION
Terrassa, Spain - FC Barcelona

It really was a fantastic trip and worth every second, we even got let onto the pitch at the end and have spotted ourselves in the croud on the highlights video! Thanks all for the well wishes, I hope you all get to your FM Teams game soon!!

Top Oss Till I Die!

WESLEY AND ME

JONNY SHARPLES

On Football Manager 2010 I took on the role of Gateshead manager. In desperate need of a striker I looked to Newcastle United, who were my feeder club. In their reserves was a young Frenchman called Wesley Ngo Baheng, who agreed to join me on loan and so started a love affair between myself and Wesley.

He finished my first season as top scorer in the Blue Square Bet Premier and in the next two seasons as we clinched promotion into League Two. That was just the start of the Ngo Baheng adventure.

Wesley went on to score in every single division and competition we played in on our rise to the Premier League, becoming Gateshead's all-time record appearance maker and goalscorer along the way.

Such was my love for him that I ordered a Gateshead replica shirt and asked the club to print 'NGO BAHENG 8' on the back. I had to specifically request this, as the option wasn't available.

I also had a shirt printed in celebration of his achievements in becoming Gateshead's all-time record goalscorer. A page on Wikipedia was also created, detailing each season, before it was removed for "fictional information based in the future". Wikipedia clearly just doesn't appreciate Football Manager.

But on November 11, 2010, Gateshead genuinely took Wesley Ngo Baheng on trial. I had predicted the future through Football Manager. Sadly the dream ends there, Wesley Ngo Baheng was never given a contract and Gateshead remain in the Blue Square Bet Premier - if only they had me in charge.

Today Wesley and I are Facebook friends, but I think he's a bit too busy to notice I have a photo of me wearing a shirt with his name on it.

> I ordered a Gateshead shirt and asked them to print NGO BAHENG 8 on the back

Ngo Baheng

TECHNICAL SUPPORT

SUKI BAHTH

My parents weren't that well off, so no Sky TV and definitely no consoles.

'CM3.exe' was basically my life. Installed on my family's first PC, it became a 24-hour job on weekends. Most kids my age were starting to discover girlfriends and starting to fights. I was signing Batistuta for Manchester United.

I also learnt the ins and outs of PCs, allowing me to understand why my PC was low on RAM; how to install additional RAM; how to install patches; how to extend I/O device cables to play without getting out of bed. It sparked my interest in PCs and the power they hold.

Which, with a few other influences, led to me graduating in IT and working for one of the largest IT vendors in the world.

An addiction? Most likely. Was that a bad thing? Never.

It sparked my interest in PCs and the power they hold

JAMES AND THE GIANT PIE

JONATHAN MARUM

I moved to Sheffield in 2007 to start my University degree and when the 2008 version of FM came out my team was Sheffield United, recently relegated to the Championship. My star player was James Beattie, who scored a glorious 37 goals in our successful promotion campaign. Unfortunately, he never had the chance to disappoint in the Premiership. After hearing of interest from Juventus he demanded to move and I was forced to sell for £8.5m by the board.

At the start of Feburary 2008 I ran into Beattie at the Devonshire Chippy in Sheffield just after midnight, in quite an inebriated state, and proceeded to tell him about how he upped and left us for the more glamorous surroundings of Turin.

I will never forget his reply, mouth full of steak and onion pie: "Why on earth did I do that lad? Can't get grub like this in Italy can you?"

No James, no you can't.

I told him how he'd left us for the more glamorous surroundings of Turin

FM PLANNED MY HONEYMOON

TIM PYKE

It was 2007 and my future wife and I had set a date for our wedding – 08-08-08. A month later, we would go on our honeymoon.

She had been looking at holidays in Spain, Greece or Portugal and I was all for it. But then came the fateful day I started beta-testing the Bulgarian league for Football Manager.

I picked a random team. That team changed the whole concept of holidaying. That team was Nesebar, in the Bulgarian Second Division West.

I grew fond of them and followed their real-life progress. Then I got curious and looked at costs for holidays in Bulgaria. I found out about the holiday resort of Sunny Beach, right next to Nesebar's football stadium and the prices were excellent. Could I convince the wife-to-be?

Yes I could. Two weeks all-inclusive was cheaper than one week half-board at any of the other locations, so it was set. September 5, 2008 I was flying out to Bulgaria. Now I needed to figure out a way to go and see Nesebar in action. A week into the honeymoon the opportunity arrived. We made some new friends out there and the girls wanted to split off to have some girlie time. I convinced the lads to go see the football. Although the wife knew I went to the football match, to this day she doesn't know I chose Bulgaria because of the team I saw play out there.

YOUTH POLICY

MARTIN HAWKINS

Since I first started playing CM, I have grown feelings for teams I have managed. On CM1 it was Crewe Alexandra, with Neil Lennon and Danny Murphy, and on CM2 I fell in love with Wigan and their Spanish trio of Jesus Seba, Roberto Martinez and Isidro Diaz.

Later in life (I am 31) I have taken an affinity towards the lower leagues in England, and I would like to think that I am the only person in Denmark who owns replica shirts from Boston United, King's Lynn and Weston-super-Mare. They aren't exactly easy to get hold of, either.

Our first child was born last summer; while we were at the hospital I put in a good shift whenever our newborn was sleeping. My girlfriend was not amused.

Evening w.

Maternity ward FM

PRIMUS INTER NERDUS

MIKE SWIFT

I attended a Magic: The Gathering tournament with my teenage son in the United States of America. I brought along my Alienware laptop computer, which I'd purchased two months earlier with the specific purpose of playing FM on it. Many of the tournament participants were aware that my computer model is designed especially for computer gaming and were quite impressed at seeing one up close and personal.

After they were done ogling the hardware, they inquired about the software. Was I playing World of Warcraft? Call of Duty? Halo? When they learned I played FM on it exclusively, they were shocked.

"You spent that much money on a gaming computer to play Football Manager? What the heck is that? "

I explained in their jargon that "It's a turn-based sports-based simulation in which I become a manager of a football club somewhere on Earth".

They weren't convinced that my money was well spent. I continued, "It's a game that has a database of 57 countries, 118 leagues, and over 350,000 players on it."

"Really? That's awesome! How do they get all the information?"

Then, I landed the detail-oriented inquisitors who spend hours researching the best playing cards to build their competitive Magic decks (sometimes spending over $1000); combinations of 60+ cards across five colors, each with unique themes and strategies, to defeat their opponents, with a hook they couldn't resist.

"Most of the database is created voluntarily by fans of the game who research the players according to approximately 26 attributes and a host of other hidden attributes. The research is then coded into the game and the players can improve or get worse depending on my choices as manager and are affected by the decisions that I make regarding their training, the match experience they are provided, and the motivational speeches I give them within the framework of the game, in matches and in the press."

"Wow! That's impressive and sounds massively detailed!"

I swelled with pride. I'd impressed this finicky crowd of gamers, many of whom were half my age.

"So, what are you doing right now?" One of them saw my word document opened up with over 100K displaying as the word count.

"I'm writing a story about it." I replied.

"You're writing a story about a computer game?" He inquired, with more than a hint of disbelief in his voice.

"Yes, I'm writing a novelisation about my career within the game and it's currently more than 100,000 words in length."

"Wow!" Then came the silence as his mind whirred in contemplation as to whether or not he should verbalize his thoughts. "What do you do with what you write?"

"I put it online in an international forum community where fellow writers share their versions of their careers in story form. We even have an awards ceremony in which people vote for their favorite stories, characters, plot lines, and best authors, including a Hall of Fame."

I waited patiently, bracing myself with the knowledge that many who play Magic: The Gathering are an eccentric lot with some rough social skills.

I didn't have to wait long before he checkmated me. "Don't take offence at this, but that's really geeky...even for nerds."

We both laughed and he returned to the next round of the tournament in which he was competing against the other 40 males who had gathered in a very small warehouse with extremely poor heating in the middle of winter with the outside temperature just below freezing playing his role-playing card game on a Friday night while wearing his winter coat, a knit cap, and fingerless gloves to sit on a steel folding chair at a wobbly card table opposite his opponent dressed in similar fashion.

Seven-A-Side

GEORGE HABERMAN

When my disk broke I went to a Friday night street football tournament with my friends, dressed in a suit, with orange slices in my lunchbox and with a notepad full of the tactics I used for my Football Manager team, which had been adapted for seven-a-side. I used all the same methods as I did on my game and we played five, won four and drew one. The people running the tournament advised me to apply for my coaching badges as they thought I had a natural talent for it.

Mike Swift's tale of a meeting of the minds between one FMer and the denizens of the murky underworld that is Magic: The Gathering mentions the work he and others undertake in novelising their Football Manager careers. Mike and lots of other great writers post on the FM Stories forum that can be found at http://community.sigames.com – we think you'll like their work.

COMMUNICATION BREAKDOWN

J JAKUBOWSKI

I'm a very emotional and tempestuous player. Once I was playing in the Champions League final and lost, conceding a goal in the last minute of extra time, despite leading 2-0 at half-time.

My reaction was to throw my cell phone at the wall. It broke, of course. The LCD stopped displaying anything and the microphone was broken too. I couldn't afford a new one and as punishment my parents refused to buy me one.

When people called me (or I called them) they wouldn't hear me, but I would hear them. When texting, I was unable to read messages, but I could type replies (some texts were gibberish because I didn't see the mistakes I made). For five months my friends called me, telling me what they wanted to say and then I texted them back. Hell on Earth.

> I threw my phone at the wall. As punishment, my parents refused to buy me a new one

ANTI-SOCIAL NETWORKING

MATTY BROADFOOT

Ever since I first purchased Championship Manager 4 and found an unknown Morten Gamst Pedersen available on loan from Tromso, I have been hooked. I told near enough anyone with ears that I had found him long before Blackburn Rovers did.

Yes, I have worn a suit when playing a final at Wembley, and yes, I have conducted mini press conferences while taking a toilet break at 2am.

However, the moment I realised it had completely taken over was during a long blown-out save as Tiverton Town of English non-league obscurity. I had flown through the leagues and finally made it to the Premiership. Throughout this save a 16-year-old striker, Ashley Barnes, on loan from my feeder club Plymouth, was banging in the goals. He scored over 500 goals in 600 appearances, even claiming the Premiership Golden Boot.

I literally became obsessed with him and this filtered over to my life outside FM when I stumbled across his Bebo social networking page. I left a 17-year-old Plymouth youth player a long-winded comment, informing him of his Tiverton exploits, giving him tips on his best position and declaring my love for him, talking as if I was a weird combination of his gaffer/stalker, something I now feel so stupid for. Although I have held back from trying to contact him since, I still look out for his name on Gilette Soccer Saturday every week.

MR BOWIE'S CHAMP MAN MASTERCLASS

HAPPY BIRTHDAY, DELE ADEBOLA

CHRIS COUPLAND

The year of the 00/01 game I felt like everybody was playing it, even the teachers would be telling everybody who the next wonderkid was.

There was one class where Mr Bowie would spend the first 25 minutes talking about how his Carlisle game was coming along. He was so pleased at finishing 17th in the Premiership with his newly-promoted side. Somebody shouted about how he should sign Tonton Zola Moukoko and he replied with a smile, "That was my first signing, he's my captain". It was easily my favourite class of the week. Luckily there were only two girls in it, I think they may have been the only reason we didn't talk Champ Man the entire time.

When I got my first part-time job, I would run through my squad in my head while working. Where did I need to improve? Who was surplus to requirements? I used to do pretend interviews about recent performances, talking about specific players.

I would make songs up for players I found, like calling Fernando Genro 'The General'. Celtic won the European Cup at Wembley and I made The Pogues 'London Girl' my fans' theme song for that season.

Writing this makes me think I went too far.

OWEN SCOTT

I remember at school (I'm 33 now) I was nicknamed Crowded House because their song Four Seasons in One Day described my Championship Manager experience.

My story is all around my hero - Dele Adebola. I started a game of Champ Man as Crewe and my obsession with Dele began. He was 19, but became the lynchpin of the side which took Europe and England by storm. Thirty-five Premier League titles in a row and numerous European titles and Dele was there for about 15 of them. I had numerous bids for him, but just couldn't sell and I let him decide when it was time to retire. At my school prom I was honoured to receive the Dele Adebola Award for Services to Football Statistics - basically a can of juice with some paper around it. My mates thought it would be a good joke and seemed gobsmacked when I was so proud to receive it.

I sent Dele a couple of birthday cards but never got any reply and have followed his career very closely. Only last season through a man I knew who knew Billy Davies, I managed to get my hands on a couple of signed photos of Dele and a signed Forest top from his time there. I remember being excited reading the 90 Minutes magazine one week when Dele was linked with a £1m move to Wimbledon, but it never came off. Who would think a schoolboy from a mining village in Scotland would grow up to idolise a Crewe teenager?

CAR CRASH TV

OLEG

I was looking forward to November 5, 2010. It was Friday, I still clearly remember, and I had pre-ordered my digital copy of Football Manager 2011.

I had to work and the routine seemed very long for me. Close to the end of the day, my friends asked me out for a beer. I refused, because I knew that FM awaited me at home. And it was a vital decision.

I got home and played for a few hours, then I had a phone call, and was informed that there had been a car accident - both of my friends were hospitalised with injuries, and the car was smashed. I can't even describe how shocked I was. Who knows, maybe this game saved my life?

VAUXHALL AND I

LEE RAE

I started university in 2006, the year of my Vauxhall Motors save. After three years battling hard in the Conference North on a shoestring budget, I managed to get promoted to the Conference. Two more seasons followed before I was promoted to League 2 following a number of shrewd signings (the best being an unknown striker by the name of Vijay Sidhu, from Coventry under-18s on a free).

Whilst in League 2, I had the opportunity to sign Rory Fallon. The New Zealand striker had had a reasonable career in the higher leagues with Plymouth and my local team, Barnsley. At 6ft 2ins I thought he would be ideal as a target man and sure enough the goals flowed.

One night I was out in Barnsley and noticed Rory across the bar. Having had a few beers, I thought it only right that I should inform the front man of his scoring exploits for me. He was delighted to hear that he was a hit on FM, however was slightly taken aback when I told him that he was banging them in for lowly Vauxhall Motors.

He was clearly hoping I was manager of Real Madrid!

MAN AND BOY

HENDERSON

Twenty years ago, give or take, me and my mate were playing Championship Manager round his house.

In those days, preparing the game between seasons took roughly four million years. You had to click the mouse a couple of times every million years or so. We did this and then walked up to the Chinese to grab a chicken chow mein. When we got back, my mate's mum said that I had to call my cousin for some reason. To cut a long story short, my dad had had a heart attack and died on a squash court. They don't tell you this over the phone, you know. You have to go to the hospital and get told face-to-face.

I never did get to eat that chicken chow mein - went cold in the car.

Anyway, fast forward 20 years and I'm in front of a laptop playing the same game. They have a 3D match-engine now. Imagine that.

When I play CM I play it hard. I take it to work, to play in my lunch break. I play it in the morning before work, I play it while the kids are going to sleep, I play it after the kids have gone to sleep.

The point I'm trying to make is this. What a gigantic waste of time. I mean, I've always known it's been a giant waste of time. It doesn't even particularly bother me that it's a waste of time. When it comes down to it, just about everything that could be considered a hobby is a waste of time. People have hobbies because they are fun, not because they are achieving a great deal.

Work is also a big waste of time.

Pretty much everything is a waste of time, when you get right down to it. Maybe some things are more worthwhile wastes than others. Not sure about that though.

When I was younger, I had great expectations of myself. I didn't know what I was going to do with life, but I was pretty sure I'd be fantastic at it. Great expectations. Low workrate. Killer combination.

If there was one thing I wouldn't have banked on doing 20 years after my old man chased his last lost cause, it would be playing Championship Manager. And yet here I am. And I'll do it again, because, ultimately, I haven't grown up one little bit from that kid with the cold chow mein. I do a half-decent impression of being a good dad. That's about the best that could be said.

Deep down I still think that taking Dover to the Championship from the Blue Square South is a worthy achievement. In an alternative life, I could get a job at Dover, gain multiple promotions, and eventually move to Roma, where I would win Serie A.

And I only went out of the Champions League because of a bug whereby if you press the space bar twice it skips the team setup screen if you have a valid lineup. I could have been the champion of Europe, you know.

Anyway. I have more time now I have kicked my addiction for another year or two. Enough time to write crap posts like this. And to think of some other ridiculous way of wasting my time.

A life of forgotten Championship Manager saves. It's not a ringing endorsement, people.

HENDERSON RESPONDED TO A POST WE MADE ON CRAPMANAGER.INFO

This is one of our favourite of the many subcultures that exist within the FM community. It was started by a band of fundamentalist zealots who were expelled from the SI forums, where they had preached their puritanical brand of gameplay to a hostile audience of non-believers.

As Henderson puts it: "I miss those days of sanctimonious self-righteousness. We educated the masses, and for that we deserve credit. We taught the Bakayoko-chasers that they were not having fun, that their achievements were worthless, and that they had failed as human beings."

This hardy group has survived almost as long as the game itself and is worth checking out for its 'careers' section, written in adherence to the rules of crap management. Games always begin in the lower leagues and players will never be named – one of the cornerstones of crap management is that there is no sharing of information: be it tactics or signings.

Crap Managers

"The devil was always Robbie Keane," said Stephen, of the former CM3 world-beater. Shortly afterwards, Cosmic Trigger posted: "I've seen R***** K**** mentioned twice now without the appropriate censoring. Remember: no tipping."

FAVOURITE PERSONNEL

STUART WARREN

Back in the CM days at school, myself and my group of friends were your typical addicts – obsessing over wonderkids, spending lessons drawing up our best XI and, when the editor came into play, adding ourselves into the game.

Ant and Ben were hooked as much as I was. It was a constant thing in our lives, as it was for countless others.

Once we finished school we all went our separate ways - Ben travelling round the world, Ant and I into very different university courses. We all kept up with CM/FM, but aside from a quick dabble in a network game, didn't see so much of each other, so the CM/FM chats and comparisons faded off.

Fast forward a couple of years - I'm looking for a summer job, Ant's dropped out of uni and Ben's been made redundant. We all go for the ultimate summer temp job - testing FM - and get it. Back together again, doing the same old thing we were doing back in school!

Fast forward a couple of years again and we're now all fully-fledged, permanent members of the SI team, living together in London. And this season we started a Sunday League football team called FC To Madeira, in honour of everyone's favourite fake player.

> We all go for the ultimate summer temp job - testing FM - and get it

Ant, Ben & Stu

Club Badge

Home Kit

/ FC To Madeira (To Madeira not pictured)

FM at the Euros

JORDI ALBA

Alba is pretty much the perfect modern-day left-wing back, with France abandoning their usual tactics to stick two defensive right-backs on him to no avail in their quarter-final clash.

In 2009 his promise has already been identified in the game, after some strong showings for the Valencia B teams.

A graduate of Barcelona's famed youth academy - without quite securing the first-team breakthrough - he sealed a £12 million return to the Camp Nou this summer, apparently turning down Manchester United in the process

FOOTBALL CRAZY?

Why it's perfectly healthy to conduct
press conferences in the shower

If you have played Champ Man or FM, you have probably had a moment
– maybe more than one – when you have questioned your own sanity.
God knows **Iain Macintosh** has, so we asked him to take one for the team
on the psychologist's coach. Wait...

> I've had girlfriends
> I haven't loved as much
> as my Uefa Cup-winning
> Southend United side

Sometimes, I worry about the effect that Football
Manager has had on my life. I've had girlfriends
I haven't loved as much as my Uefa Cup-winning
Southend United side (CM97/98), friends that
I haven't seen as much as I saw my Nottingham
Forest reserves (CM01/02). Why is it that I've never
stayed up until 3am to write a book, but I did it on
numerous occasions to guide Welling out of the
Conference South (FM07)?

I decided that it was time to go and see a man
who could give me some answers. Dr Simon
Moore, Principal Lecturer in Psychology at London
Metropolitan University and a renowned expert
in the effects of gaming on the human condition.
If anyone can tell me whether or not I've got
a serious, serious problem, it's him.

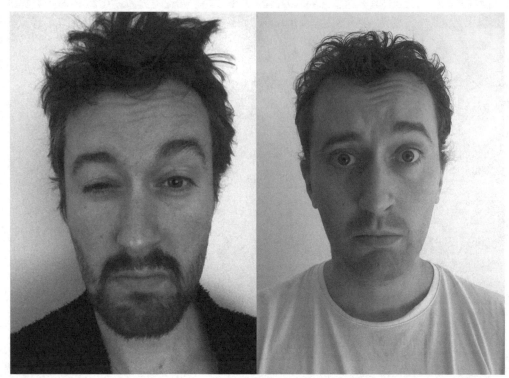

/ Iain Macintosh before and after 20 years of addiction – proof that FM is good for your health?

Iain Macintosh – Hello, Doctor. Thank you for seeing me at such short notice.

    Simon Moore – No problem at all, Iain.

IM – You see... Actually, should I be laying down for this?

    SM – If it makes you feel better.

IM – You know, I really think it will. (lies down) Oh yes, that's lovely.

    SM – Now, what seems to be the problem?

IM – Well, Doctor, it's like this. I've been playing the Football Manager games for 20 years. Since the very first one, the one with the picture of an angry man on the box, came out I've spent hours and hours and hours of my life, tinkering with make-believe football teams, playing with tactics, scouting and recruiting new players. When I think about what I could have achieved in my life, the languages I could have learned, the places I could have seen, it really does break my heart. At some point, I'm going to be on my death bed, surrounded by family members, gently ebbing away into the next plane of existence and all I'm going to be able to think about is the fact that I must have spent a cumulative total of six unbroken months playing a computer game. But you know the worst thing?

SM – *Go on...*

IM – I'm actually a football journalist. I have a press pass and everything. Within reason, and dependent on travel budgets, I can watch any football match in the country and get paid to do so. I'm basically spending all of my free time doing something which is pretty much an extension of my day job. Am I weird?

SM – *Eeeerm...*

IM – Oh dear, that's not a good start.

SM – *You're not playing the same one are you? The same one with a picture of an angry man on the box?*

IM – Oh God, no. No, I've bought every new one when it's been released. I'm not locked in 1992.

SM – *But you like the concept, you like the micro-management?*

IM – I do, I really do. I love taking over a team and assessing the squad. I like to assemble a backroom staff, prepare a coaching routine, get the youngsters mentored by senior pros, practise set-pieces, deploy scouts, everything. And then I never just play with the first team. I'll always control the reserves and the youth teams, just to make sure that there's progression in the club. And that's the strangest thing. I'm not a precise man in any other walk of life. My tax records are all over the place, my diary is written on my arm in biro, I'm forever losing notepads. But when I get on Football Manager, suddenly I become the most meticulous man in the world. Everything is planned and prepped, the future is mapped out.

SM – *When you play the game, how do you feel?*

IM – Genuinely?

SM – *Genuinely.*

IM – I feel like a God.

SM – *Really?*

IM – I feel like a God, sat astride a mountain, staring down at the mortals as they scurry like ants, desperate to do my bidding, fearful of my wrath. Is that weird? That is weird, isn't it?

SM – *Eeeerm...*

IM – I don't like the way you draw out your 'erms'

SM – *Sorry. It's not weird that you don't do these things in real life. Control freaks don't control every part of their lives. If you think about work, for example, some people are not control freaks at work because they are unable to manipulate people in that sense. But they might be in their own home, with cleanliness, or where the remote control is kept. But if you change the environment, you can change the behaviour. You must feel you have more control in this Football Manager environment.*

IM – But I'm a football journalist and I have been for six years. You'd think I'd have no need to immerse myself in this pretend world of football because I'm in the real one.

SM – *Yes, but only to a certain extent. You're not in it, you're alongside it. You're on the outside looking in. Your influence is limited.*

IM – Ah, you've seen my contacts book. Well, I say book. It's more of a pamphlet.

SM – *You don't really control the day to day mechanics of real football, or the way the real teams perform. But you do in the game.*

IM – Do you think that's why my need to play has intensified in recent years?

SM – *Maybe... Maybe that's a function of what you do. Perhaps influence is what you feel you lack and this game gives it to you in great quantity.*

IM – OK. What is it about always wanting one more game, always wanting one more match? Why am I sometimes sat downstairs on my sofa at 1am, my living room illuminated only by the glow of my laptop as I push deep into the night in pursuit of a pretend trophy?

SM – *Well, that's the same with lots of gamers and indeed lots of addictions. Think about horse racing fans always wanting one more race, gamblers unable to walk away from a fruit machine.*

IM – God, is it that bad? Is it that closely linked with other addictions?

SM – *Yep. Some people are addicted to basic principles or linear relationships. You press 'a' and 'b' happens. You have a drink and you feel good. They like that simplicity. Then there are lot of people who like the complexities of other relationships. With this sort of game there are so many possibilities, so many permutations. You could literally play Football Manager a hundred times and have a different result every time. You are also obviously addicted to this kind of 'deity' analogy that you eluded to earlier. Your addiction is built around a 'what happens if I do this to them?' principle.*

IM – So not only do I think I'm a God, but you think I'm also a vengeful, wrathful God?

SM – *Well, not entirely. You want your team to perform well. That's your aim.*

IM – But if I was the kind of person who dropped players repeatedly, fined them, transfer–listed them, then I'd be a vengeful God?

Simon Moore

SM – *Exactly. Your personality is going to come out somehow in the game itself. Are you impulsive in the transfer market?*

IM – No. I'm quite impulsive in real–life markets, especially if cheese is involved, but not on Football Manager. I always make sure that my signings are the result of thorough scouting and extensive deliberation.

SM – *You see, you're very concerned about how you do in the game, that's your motivation. You can't talk about personality without talking about motivation. You want to perform well, but it's also integral to the fact that you enjoy it so much. You don't want to spoil the enjoyment by failing to put in the investment. If you're not winning, you're not having fun.*

IM – Is it not a little concerning that in real life I'm reckless and impulsive, but in Football Manager I'll micromanage and plan?

SM – *Well, it just goes to show that you're not stable in your personality, doesn't it?*

IM – Really?

SM – *Yes. Don't worry, that sounds a lot worse than it is. It's a good thing.*

IM – It is?

SM – *Instability is good. Not reckless instability. You don't want to be murdering someone with an axe one day and then acting normal the next day.*

IM – I'm not an axe murderer.

SM – *I didn't say that you were.*

IM – I just want to clarify that.

SM – *Of course, of course. What I mean is that your personality is flexible. It's going to be linked to greater issues of survival. If you adopted the same persona, the same characteristics, you wouldn't be able to adapt to changing situations. If I wired you up for the day, I'd be able to show that you had spoken differently to different people, that you were acting differently, more or less confident, according to different scenarios. You're simply adapting your personality for survival in the game. In real life, you can behave as you do because the ramifications are not especially dramatic. You're untidy, but the world doesn't end because of it. You're impulsive, but I assume it hasn't caused your life to break down in any way? But you know that if you don't plan in Football Manager, you'll be less likely to win and winning is what gives you pleasure, which in turn is what drives the addiction.*

IM – Oh.

SM – *It's a reinforcement, a positive reinforcement. Your work only pays your bills, Football Manager delivers hits of pleasure. So it's not a surprise that you'll act differently.*

IM – This isn't going to look good to prospective employers, is it?

SM – *It's perfectly normal. You're going to get more motivated by things that make you feel good than things that you have to do.*

PHILOSOPHY FOOTBALL

After many years during which I saw many things, what I know most surely about morality and the duty of man I owe to sport.

Camus was an author and philosopher, and also a goalkeeper with a bravery rating of 20, before contracting tuberculosis in 1930, at the age of 17, an infectious condition that was incurable (send home from training). He was an ardent opponent of nihilism and as such would have found value in a life lived vicariously through a top-quality management simulation.

Albert Camus

IM – Do you think it's a little sad that micromanaging a pretend football team gets me off more than, say, a big fat line of cocaine?

SM – Not at all. That's just how motivation works. It's like the way that money motivates some and not others, it's personal. Football Manager is what appeals to you. Not big fat lines of cocaine. Which is probably a good thing on balance, I'd say.

IM – Ok. But is it a bad thing that I occasionally imagine conversations with my players?

SM – No, because that's integral to the whole experience. It's the immersion that appeals to you, that's what draws you in. I've heard of people giving speeches in empty rooms, shaking hands with doorknobs and pretending it's a member of the Royal Family. You're just keeping the situation alive, doing what you need to do to keep the dream going. As long as you're not hurting anyone else, it's fine.

IM – What about doing press conferences in my head?

SM – That's fine too. In fact, for you, it's even more normal because that's an environment that you know well, so it's easy for you to imagine it.

IM – Well, this is all very encouraging. Have you ever encountered people who aren't normal? People who have taken these things too far?

SM – Oh yes. You have people who have seen their health fade, whose personal relations have broken down, who haven't been able to break away long enough to do work. But these are extremes. There are always going to be some people who struggle with addiction, but that's the same with any kind of stimulus.

IM – Isn't it worrying that there are so many similarities between Football Manager addiction and, say, alcohol addiction?

SM – Addiction is addiction.

IM – So my 'addiction' to Football Manager is actually a genuine, 20–year addiction?

SM – Yes.

IM – Wow... I think that's actually longer than Eric Clapton did cocaine.

SM – The health risks aren't as great with Football Manager.

IM – Someone should have mentioned that to Clapton.

SM – It's possible that his music may have suffered.

IM – (sings) Layla. You've got me on my knees, Layla. Distracted from friendlies, Layla. I'm begging Darling for you to do my coaching routiiiiiines!

[SILENCE]

SM – Please don't EVER do that again.

IM – Sorry.

SM – [shudders] Anyway, anything like this, anything that you enjoy will get your endorphins flowing. That will amplify the positive feeling. It's all down to cognition; whatever you believe is a positive stimulus will have that effect. Your subconscious enjoys Football Manager, it enjoys winning, it enjoys the alternative reality that you create. This, for want of a better phrase, is your drug.

IM – Gosh. So, is admitting that I have a problem the first step to recovery?

SM – Is it a problem? Or is it just something you enjoy? Is it negatively impacting anything in your life?

IM – Well, sometimes my wife gets offended if she's watching a Jennifer Aniston movie and I play it on my laptop on the sofa next to her.

SM – Well, you've got a problem.

IM – I have?

SM – Yes, Jennifer Aniston movies are almost exclusively awful.

IM – It's not just me, is it?

SM – Nope.

IM – Every film is the same. She's a gorgeous singleton who, for inexplicable reasons, just cannot find a man and she has a friend who is also gorgeous, but in a less obvious way, and she is mostly there to make sardonic jokes. Then she meets someone who is ABSOLUTELY unsuitable for her and they have arguments that become increasingly heated until something draws them together and they kiss, only to swiftly jeopardise the whole affair on a point of principle before a race against time brings them together forever.

SM – I've actually got real work to do, you know.

IM – Sorry.

SM – So, Football Manager isn't causing you any real problems? You play it up until a certain point and then you stop playing it?

IM – Yes. But sometimes that certain point is 1am and I'm up again at 6am.

SM – Well, you know what you can and can't do. I take it that you haven't failed to get up at 6am, that you haven't failed to do what you've had to do the next day?

IM – No. I've just been a bit tired.

SM – Well, that's fine. The point is that you're still doing what you need to do. In fact, your brain might be thinking, 'I had lots of fun last night playing Football Manager, now let's do some work'.

IM – It usually tells me to make a cup of tea and a bacon sandwich first, but yes, I see your point.

SM – That's fine as well. If you cut the fat off.

IM – That's a good tip. So basically, if it's not a problem, it's not a problem?

SM – Essentially, yes. I mean, if you're denying it to yourself and it is a problem, if you're not meeting people, if you're not eating properly, if you're not doing any work, then it's a different matter, but this isn't the case, is it?

IM – No! This is wonderful news. I feel like I've had a great weight lifted off my shoulders!

SM – I'm happy to have helped. You know, games are often demonised, especially the violent ones, but that's not fair. We know what they're about, gamers know what they're about. You do what you must to progress in the game.

IM – What is it that sends some people to fighty games and some people to football games? Why do some people want to slay a dragon, while others just want to win a pretend trophy?

> Games are often demonised, particularly violent ones, but that's not fair. We know what they are about

SM – All games are about play. We don't stop playing at the age of 12. Play is integral to psychology. It lets you rehearse, it gives you enjoyment, it lets you do things you wouldn't ordinarily do. Video games are extensions of stories.

IM – But what is it that attracts some people to fighting a dragon and some people to a statistic-loaded football database that is essentially an exercise in human resources? Surely we'd all rather fight a dragon?

SM – Would you?

IM – Well, yes.

SM – I wouldn't, I'd rather coach a football team. It's safer.

IM – Not if it's Millwall. What I'm trying to say is, are there certain personality types that will be drawn to Football Manager?

SM – No, I wouldn't say so. I've done some research on this and personality types don't necessarily pick specific games. There's more of a relationship with their personality and how they play the game. Do they use melee weapons or spells, are they reckless drivers or careful drivers? These traits can correlate with personality. How that relationship manifests itself is completely random. Some cautious people are reckless in games, some reckless people, like you, are cautious. It's possible that you're living up to an ideal that perhaps you can't achieve in real life.

It's possible that you're living up to an ideal that you can't achieve in real life

IM – Woah. That's pretty deep.

    SM – That's what I do.

IM – So, to recap: I play Football Manager because I like it and my subconscious likes it. I'm cautious because that's what my subconscious believes is the best way to prosper, and therefore how I'll like it more. I hold press conferences in my head because it adds to the enjoyment and the best bit, it's not a problem because it's not a problem. My life is still very much intact.

    SM – Precisely.

IM – Well, that's great. Now, can you do me a favour? Can you call my wife and tell her everything you've just told me?

    SM – Get out.

I hold press conferences in my head because it adds to the enjoyment. My life is still very much intact

---

GAME CHANGER

How FM has altered the way
we think about football

The Football Manager franchise has had a profound effect on millions of lives, enchanting and entrapping players for 20 years. However, there have also been times when its tendrils have spread from the alternate reality it creates to the actual reality it imitates.

BALA CHALLENGE

Bala Town
Welsh Premier League.

A small semi-professional outfit in the Welsh Premier League, BALA TOWN were the very definition of 'obscure'. At least, as commercial director GARETH MOON explains, until FM2011 was released.

We didn't know what was happening at first, we only knew that our website s were going through the roof and that we were getting a stream of messages on Twitter asking for our current tactics and advice on our players. Confused, we asked them where they were all coming from and they told us that we were the subject of a competition on a podcast. Apparently, the show's presenters had challenged their listeners to take Bala Town as far as they could in five seasons on Football Manager 2011 and then report back for prizes.

We're only a small Welsh Premier League club in a town with a population of slightly over 2000, so to have that kind of interest was unprecedented. I'd never played the game before, but some of the younger ones around the club had, so we had to ask them what it was all about. It was very strange and the players found it very odd.

The manager wasn't sure about it at first, I think he thought someone was taking the mickey out of us, but once we explained it he seemed quite positive. I don't think he's played the game himself yet though, I think he's got enough on his hands with the real thing.

We thought it was all great and we invited the four winners down to the club for a day out and a guided tour. They went back and blogged very positively about their trip, which furthered the interest. We've had more people coming to games, especially from outside the region and there's now a thriving Bala Town community on Twitter. They've even sponsored the match ball this season.

We've had increased press coverage, increased merchandise sales, we've had producers approaching us with new products to sell online, we've had representatives from other clubs and even other sports approaching us, asking how we've generated such a buzz. It's been amazing.

When the new game came out, the players were straight on it, wanting to check out their stats. I think they find it quite flattering to be a part of such a global phenomenon. And then, of course, we got another surge of interest around the world as people tried to win the league with us. We've got one lad in America who keeps emailing to tell us his progress, letting us know that he's got us into the Champions League.

It hasn't raised expectations or attracted negative attention whatsoever. It's been entirely positive, entirely beneficial and it all stems from that Football Manager competition.

DEMANDING TIMES

Rory Smith
Football Writer, The Times.

Now a football writer for The Times, RORY SMITH discovered Football Manager in his teens and it helped develop his thirst for knowledge.

My mate John, who had a computer before me, had Championship Manager 2 and as soon as I saw it, I wanted it. I was gagging for it. Finally, I got CM97/98 and that's where it all began. I had to use the computer in my dad's office, so I'd get my homework out of the way every night, go across at 7pm and would usually have to be dragged out of there at midnight.

I'm a Liverpool fan, but I don't think I ever actually played as Liverpool. I preferred to take random foreign teams. The Belgian league was as exotic as it got then, so I'd start there and see where it would take me. I did themed games where I'd only allow myself to buy Spanish players, or Croatian players, things like that. I think I was always relatively in control of my addiction, and it was an addiction, but I've pulled a few all-nighters in my time. Celta Vigo? I won 16 straight Spanish titles with them. That cost me a lot of nights out ... and four or five friends ... and at least one girlfriend, come to think of it. All the way from there to 2005, I played that and Pro-Evolution Soccer and nothing else. Then I started at The Mirror as a news reporter and a combination of the demands of my job and the game's growing complexity meant that I lost the time to really indulge in things like preparing set-piece training programmes.

I discovered the game when I was watching Italian football and reading World Soccer, when I'd started to discover a world of football beyond my national boundaries, and it really tapped into that. It was educational as well. Football Manager gave me an incredible base of knowledge of European football and you can see from Twitter and elsewhere that it's still having that effect on people now. I reckon if you did a survey of all the bloggers and up-and-coming writers that specialise in South American or European football, most of them will have started out with this game.

I do think it can be crucial in building knowledge, especially now when readers are far more demanding of journalists. There's a basic level of knowledge, especially of rising stars around the globe, that you're expected to have. My interest in European football came first, but my becoming literate in it can probably be attributed to Football Manager. In fact, since I stopped playing it in 2005, my wider knowledge has probably gone down.

It does have its drawbacks. I'm occasionally berated by readers if I suggest that a certain player from, say, a Turkish league is on the shortlist of an English club. I'll get angry tweets claiming that he's not fast enough for the Premier League. You think, how on earth can you possibly have a well-formed opinion on a player in a league that isn't even televised in this country? And then you realise it's probably because he has a pace of 11 and not 19 on the latest FM.

And sometimes, the alternative world of the game can intrude on real life. Every year, you see these names of obscure potential transfer targets popping up on the forums with whispers about impending moves from 'insiders'. Then journalists, who don't make things up and have to do their job, will check it out with the agent, just in case. Invariably the agent will be delighted to see his client's name linked with the club, will happily drum up the interest and from there and – who knows? – the move might even come to pass. It's life imitating art and it makes you wonder at how much power the makers of this game have at their disposal.

Ultimately though, its legacy can be seen in the progress of other games. The Fifa and Pro-Evo games now have far more club and player details than they ever did before. Football Manager changed the industry and it's helped increase an entire generation's knowledge of the game.

Simon Banoub

STATS
ENTERTAINMENT

Opta
Simon Banoub, Marketing Director.

For the past 20 years, Opta have made their name in statistics and marketing director SIMON BANOUB believes that the rise of Football Manager has helped identify the market.

I've been playing Football Manager since the original came out with all the made-up player names. I think its success has taken a similar path to our own. It's gone from cultish appeal to international recognition and we've gone from a handful of employees operating out of one office to a multi-national company working out of offices all over the world.

There was a time when football coverage was far more basic, when people feared what they perceived to be an 'Americanisation' of sport, with statistics taking over everything. We're getting to the stage now where you'll be laughed out of the room if you don't understand the impact they have on the sport. A lot of that is down to this game.

Football Manager's strength in the early days was that it was like an early internet. While the traditional media could only offer up a few pages at the back of the paper, the game had limitless pages of information to be consumed. It played its part in laying the ground for companies like ourselves. Early sites like Sportal or TEAMtalk could come at the market with stats pages and people who had played the games weren't surprised or taken aback by what they saw. They had that feature set in mind already, so it opened the door for a new wave of media.

I think our inner geek, if you like, has always been there. You'll always find people who unashamedly love the statty side of football. They're the people who gravitate towards games like Football Manager and, in turn, towards the really in-depth things that we do.

We hear stories of people using Opta stats to help them in their Football Manager games and we hear of it the other way round as well, with people discovering players on the game and coming to us to find out more. Eden Hazard was a case in point, we had lots of questions about him. It's a well known phenomenon these days that future superstars will pop up on the game before they hit the mainstream.

It might sound daft, but I really believe that there's a movement to get more in-depth coverage of sport. We're at the head of it, with Football Manager, other media outlets and numerous bloggers, all driving stats and sophistication further into the national consciousness.

Of course, now I've got kids, my days of playing the full version are over. I play it on iPad now, where it's more like the old game I obsessed about in my youth. Sometimes, too many stats can be a problem.

SKY'S THE LIMIT

Andy Burton
Reporter, Sky News.

ANDY BURTON is a touchline reporter for Sky Sports, and has found that the lines between reality and make-believe can sometimes go blurry.

I'm not into computer games, really. I think I stopped playing them when I gave up on Super Mario Kart and discovered girls. But my girlfriend bought Football Manager 2009 for me and she regretted it almost immediately. She mentioned it to her friends and they told her about people failing their degrees and losing their jobs, going completely off the rails. She started Googling it and found the story about it being cited in a divorce case. But by that point it was too late. I was in.

I do the Premier League, because that's what I do with Sky. It's too much for my brain to drop all the way down the levels, because I don't know football inside-out down there. I've heard of people taking Vauxhall Motors to the Champions League. I'm not that deep into it, but where I know the subject matter, that's where I like it. I've got a game going now with Tottenham and I'm 26 seasons in. Seriously. I'm so deep in that it's 2036 in this game and I just won the quadruple. I haven't bought the new one because I can't bring myself to end this game.

When I used to do that transfer stuff on Sky, I must admit I have checked out a player to see what attributes they have. It's like Eden Hazard, I'm sure everyone's known about him for ages because he's so good on the game. I'd rather look there first than Google. Sometimes though, the lines get blurred.

I signed Tal Ben Haim for Burnley from Portsmouth and I was really deep into the game when I was sent to Fratton Park to cover a game for Sky. I was stood in the tunnel, the players were walking in from the warm-up, and Ben Haim walked past me. I was confused. I didn't know what was weird, I couldn't put my finger on it, but as he walked past me, I suddenly said, "What are you doing here?" He looked at me as if I was mad. And then I realised it was because I had him in Football Manager and I'd just got used to him being my captain at Burnley. It was mental. For a moment I couldn't figure out what was going on.

I've had other games where I'll set myself challenges, where I'll only sign players whose phone numbers I've got on my phone, or something like that. I know a lot of players, but that really exposed some flaws in my contact list that I then had to sort out. I went out for a few drinks with Steven Taylor recently and I was telling him about it. He's got the iPad version, but I told him that's not the same. I also told him that he'd been a bit of a p***k recently. "You what?" he said.

> It was mental.
> For a moment I couldn't figure out what was going on.

Andy Burton

I told him I'd been trying to sign him for ages, but he kept holding out for more money. I got him in the end and I'm still giving him updates now on how well he's getting on for me. I think he likes the ego boost. For them it must be weird, seeing how their lives could pan out.

If someone's giving me a hard time in real life, or I've got an on-going annoyance with someone for shooting me down in an interview, and they're struggling in my game, I'll put the boot in, I'll crank up the pressure and click the button that says 'Well, that's football. You've got to get results'.

It's an incredible game, but it will never be able to reproduce the pressure the real-life managers are put under. I spoke to Alan Curbishley when he was in the running for the England job and he was saying, "If I get it, I'll have to take my kids out of school". A few bad results, a few tough games for these guys and the mood turns. And there's some lunatics out there. Some of the stuff that Harry Redknapp and Arsene Wenger get, it's horrible. In the last few years, football managers have become more hardened to the pressure and the abuse. That's the one thing this game could never replicate.

Tony Jameson

FRINGE PLAYER

Tony Jameson
Comedian, Newcastle.

TONY JAMESON is a comedian based in Newcastle. He is writing a show based on his FM addiction that he plans to take to the 2013 Edinburgh Festival.

It's only just dawned on me that I've spent 20 years of my life playing Football Manager. I've gone from days spent at school discussing the signing of Marc Collis and Ferah Orosco. I revelled in the unbridled joy of my beloved Aston Villa signing Nii Lamptey, only to discover that he never fully lived up to the hype that surrounding him on the game. I've seen players I've signed as youngsters on the game become the best players in the world in real life. A friend and I bought Urawa Reds shirts with 'Ono' on the back, after signing Shinji Ono in separate games. We even supported Japan in the 2004 World Cup, such was his influence on us.

I've also become so involved in the games, that in their current incarnation, I've walked into the kitchen at home to be confronted by my partner asking 'what's wrong with you, you look quite confused?', only for me to reply, 'I'm trying to think of what to say in this press conference that isn't going to make me sound like a dick.'

I think it's safe to say that Football Manager has definitely taken over my life.

My crowning achievement was my career game with Blyth Spartans. I've heard of people taking a club from the Blue Square to the Premier League title, and often wondered if I'd a) have the patience, b) the backing of the board, and c) the time to undertake such a challenge. Thankfully, doing stand-up comedy, free time is something I'm blessed with. I'll often sit down to write a new routine, and more often than not find myself loading up my saved game after believing I can have 'just one game and then get back to work.' Suffice to say, I usually find myself playing the game all day at the expense of my material.

I eventually got Blyth Spartans into the Premier League. I celebrated the way any man would, by popping the champagne I had in my fridge, and then got told off by my partner as we were 'saving that for a special occasion' (we got engaged two weeks later and I still hadn't replaced the champagne).

Every season we were improving until one season, we reached the FA Cup final. It was time to don my best suit and set sail (metaphorically) to Wembley. We won on penalties against Chelsea – my first major trophy. I felt the need to celebrate, so I booked myself onto a City Tour bus the next day to give myself an open-top bus ride of Newcastle to celebrate. I even took the laptop and a small trophy with me.

The following year, something just clicked with the playing squad, and I led the club to the Premier League title. The adulation of winning the title was easily the proudest moment of my life. I hadn't realised the impact this would have on my career. When Steve McClaren got sacked by Nottingham Forest, my mate Jim announced on TV that I would be interested in applying for the job. I actually felt the need to tweet the show to 'distance myself from these malicious rumours as I was more than happy at Croft Park'.

However, this wasn't the only real life job I was linked with. At Christmas, Blyth Spartans sacked their manager, so I genuinely believed it was my destiny to step up to the plate and apply for the job.

The problem with this game, is that you lose all sense of reality playing it. Even still, I genuinely thought that given my achievements with Blyth Spartans that I'd at least be given an interview. Even if was always going to be a no, I thought they'd see the funny side of it. They didn't, and I received a fairly damning reply as to why I wasn't suitable for the job. They cited my 'lack of genuine experience' as the main reason for not hiring me, and there was also a fairly lengthy rationale for not renaming the behind-the-goal stand, 'The Tony Jameson Stand'.

I felt a little disappointed by their decision to not even interview me, but after an email conversation with the FA, I can confirm that 'it is not possible to use Football Manager as a way of attaining accreditation of prior learning in order to obtain a recognised coaching badge'. Oh well. I guess it's back to the drawing board for me.

This experience touched me in a way I never thought. So much so, that it's even inspired me to write an Edinburgh Fringe show about it which I'm hoping to perform in 2013. Ha'way the Spartans! Here's to another 20 years.

Football tactics, formations, diagrams, chalkboards and graphs – in partnership with Betfair

| Home | Euro 2012 | Match Analysis ▾ | Match Reviews | Chalkboards | Players | Graphs | General Articles | Past features ▾ | ZM Elsewhere |

ABOUT ZM • UPCOMING • BIBLIOGRAPHY • COMMENTS • ZM ELSEWHERE • DIAGRAMS • LINKS • GLOSSARY • FAQ / CONTACT • VIDEO • SUBSCRIBE

Latest Story

Spain 0-0 Portugal: Portugal upset Spain's rhythm but fail to record a shot on target

June 28, 2012

Spain defeated Portugal on penalties after a 0-0 draw.

Vicente del Bosque surprisingly named Alvaro Negredo as his lone striker, meaning Cesc Fabregas dropped to the bench. The rest of the side was as expected.

Paulo Bento was forced to change his striker, with Helder Postiga injured. As already announced, Hugo Almeida replaced him.

A difficult game to summarise – Portugal pressed well in midfield, broke up Spain's passing and restricted the number of opportunities del Bosque's side had. However, they lacked a goal threat of their own, and then Spain were the better side in extra time.

Read more »

SEARCH ZM

Google Custom Search
Search

HEADLINES

TALKING TACTICS

Michael Cox
Creator of zonalmarking.net.

An increased demand for tactical discourse enabled MICHAEL COX, the creator of zonalmarking.net, to move from blogger to professional football analyst. And Football Manager helped.

I think I first played one of the Football Manager games back in 1999. I'd been aware of them before, but we always had a crap computer, so it couldn't support the data. It's been a while now since I played it, but you can see how it's influenced so much of modern media. The statistical data in the games, the attributes, the positioning, it was phenomenal. The way that everything was determined by numbers. If it is possible to collect statistics and data about absolutely everything, then you could probably recreate the game of football quite accurately and they get closer every year.

I think football fans are far more sophisticated now than they ever used to be. We've seen a growth in serious analysis of football recently, something I've been desperate to see for years. Cricket was about 10 years ahead of football in that respect. I always hoped that football would catch up, and it did so eventually, with things like The Guardian's chalkboards.

There's an increasing and widespread familiarity with foreign teams and leagues that has come, in part at least, from the success of these games. There are other factors, of course, such as improved coverage on television and internet streaming, but a lot of the tactical familiarity and the knowledge of names comes from Football Manager.

I've spoken to a few people who feel that the game is too complicated, but when I last played it, it looked fine. I liked the way that you could use sliders to set tactics, that you didn't need FA coaching badges to organise your teams. I think it does football very well. It is, after all, a very simple game in some respects and very complex in others.

It does have its drawbacks. I do occasionally get feedback on my articles from people who base their opinions of real-life players on their Football Manager versions. That can be risky, even though the scouting on the games is very thorough and they do often get players bang on. Tactically, as well, you wonder how far it can go. People in football are always innovating, always searching for a new edge. Can you do that on this game or will it just look on unorthodox thinking unfavourably?

I can't play it now. I always remember this Jack Dee joke about service stations and the sight of men taking a break from driving by playing arcade driving games. I think it would just be too sad to take a break from writing about football to playing it. Plus, there's always the chance that it would pollute things, that I might get mixed up between the game and real life.

However, you still have to admire the fact that there is something out there appealing to real football fans. Too much gets directed to this 'laddish' ideal, there's too much shallow stuff like Soccer AM out there. Football, when you think about it, really is quite a geeky pastime.

Jonathan Wilson

PYRAMID OF POWER

Jonathan Wilson
Tactical Guru, Inverting The Pyramid.

JONATHAN WILSON has been hailed as a tactical guru since the release of his seminal work Inverting The Pyramid and honed his skills on the older versions of the game.

I first discovered Football Manager back in the early 1980s. Yes, the original Kevin Toms version. I loved it, as I did so many of the games that followed it. The early Championship Manager games were extraordinarily addictive. Those games were what passed for a social life for me, back in the day. I actually did the stats for Sunderland in CM2, you know. That's why Richard Ord is so massively overrated.

I wouldn't say that the games got me into tactics. I'd been fascinated by that side of the game since I was very young. I'd pore over the Ladybird World Cup books and diligently prepare my Subbuteo team for battle with my father. I was always interested in football and how it worked, but those games certainly enhanced my understanding of tactics. They enabled me to experiment, rather more than you could with, say, Kick Off 2. You were forced to sit back and watch, you couldn't take control with a joystick.

They also enabled me to live out fantasies. I've always been interested in Eastern European football and it was wonderful to be able to sign Krasimir Balakov for Sunderland, playing him in the hole behind Don Goodman and Phil Gray. I'm telling you, that would have worked in real life.

Quite apart from anything else, Football Manager has given people a new vocabulary. Now when you see someone saying that Manchester United need a new DMC, you know exactly what they mean. When they say Chelsea need an AM R/L, you know what they're talking about. It's a shorthand for a new generation of football fan.

In recent years, the intelligent football market has boomed. It started with Italia 90, then with Euro 96. You had books like Football Against The Enemy and Fever Pitch. Football Manager has been a huge part of that, and it's led to the development of the intelligent football fan and the market they provide. Blizzard, my quarterly football magazine, exists thanks largely to a social development that Football Manager helped to facilitate. A lot of people say that they read Inverting the Pyramid and then experimented with the formations on the game. I love that. Someone was even doing a blog where he worked through a season going through all the formations, 1-2-7, to 2-3-5 to W-M and so on. Of course, it failed dramatically because the players you want for a 1-2-7 are quite different to the ones you need for 4-5-1, but it's fascinating to see these kinds of experiments going on. Football Manager has given people more of an insight into the way that football works. If you play the game, you know that possession statistics are not everything. You know about weak spots, high defensive lines, offside traps. In a way, that's helped.

There's nothing better than writing something abstract and having people take the theory and put it into practice. When people tweet me and say that they've done that on the game, or even better, that they've done it with a Sunday league side, that's incredibly gratifying. If playing Football Manager enables people to conceptualise some of the things I write about, well, that's just fantastic.

Peter Sleeman

SCREEN SAVER

Peter Sleeman
Screenwriter

FM: The Movie? It might be closer than you think. PETER SLEEMAN wrote a screenplay based on the game and was soon fighting off bidders for his work as if it was Kennedy Bakircioglu and he was the manager of Hammarby in 2001.

I'm not actually an FM player, but it still managed to steal a fair chunk of my life.

I work in the computer game industry, but if I could do anything else, I'd be a writer and I used to always get told to 'write what you know'. I would start scripts and then never finish them. This idea was probably triggered by an article on FM and the fact that my team, Plymouth Argyle, were rubbish at the time. I thought, 'what would happen if a kid who was good at Football Manager ended up managing his local team?'

I worked on ideas about how it would start. The team is doing badly at the bottom of their league, getting thumped, and the chairman is looking around for new investment. The team is in effect, Plymouth – that is where they were at that point in the 1990s. Then I thought about things like the kid having to go to school and him discovering that it's hard to deal with adults one-to-one when you are young.

I went from never having finished anything to a completed screenplay in four weeks. I entered it in a competition and I was invited to a producers' course run by Screen South where a famous script consultant Christopher Vogler was positive about it. After that, I sold the script to a South African producer based in the United States – not for very much money. They renewed after a year but with so many options couldn't get the finance together.

The company I worked for went in to administration, so I ended up starting my own publishing company for games and iPhone apps. I kept on writing in the background and I posted on Ink Tip (an online screenwriters' forum) and responded to a lead looking for a script about football. I thought it was a shot to nothing, so I sent my script. A month later I got a call, from Wayne Godfrey, who runs a production company called The Fyzz: "You sent me your script and I love it!". He was a reasonably successful producer, and had worked with Mackenzie Crook on Three and Out.

He was working with an American guy who had been looking for sports movies so we struck a deal but again, despite much interest initially - we even had it read by the likes of Dreamworks - nothing concrete has emerged.

Wayne and I are continuing to look for funding for it. It's a story that everyone I have pitched it to understands in a moment. I am convinced one day it will get picked up and made. It's "Bend it Like Beckham for gamers", a classic story that a lot of people would want to watch.

Daniel Dawkins

CAPTAINS OF INDUSTRY

Daniel Dawkins
Editor-in-chief, Future Publishing.

DANIEL DAWKINS, Editor-in-chief of three Future Publishing gaming magazines, knows better than anyone the effect that Football Manager has had on the gaming industry.

I didn't discover Football Manager until 2006. A colleague was obsessed with it, and kept badgering me to give it a go. In the end, he left a copy on my desk with a note saying 'Try it for an hour'. I did and – despite initial bewilderment – soon saw my crude strategies affecting results. Within a week, I was playing four hours a day. Within a month, I'd 'borrowed' a work laptop to play it everywhere I went. At the height of my addiction, I'd covered my work computer in Post-it notes, scrawled with tactical permutations and lists of South American midfielders.

I'd even pretend to go to bed, then sneak away from my girlfriend on all fours using a noiseless weight distribution technique I'd dubbed 'the spider'. She told me I needed to see a doctor.

It was one of the first mainstream titles to harness the powerful and addictive mechanics of Role Playing Games (RPGs) – ie a persistent universe of statistical variables requiring constant attention. In 2012, every big game is an RPG – and not just literally, like fantasy adventure Skyrim. Call of Duty's success is due to its complex XP and online ranking system, while FIFA makes £80m a year through its stat-chasing, card-collecting, Ultimate Team mode.

FM's addiction lies in its interlinked density of feedback-response loops, almost like a stack of cards. Simple decisions are layered upon each other, until you're terrified of making minute changes – or baffled why dramatic decisions aren't having the impact you'd hoped. Trying to 'see through the matrix' is a core part of FM's appeal, trying to deduce the variables that really matter and how they interlink. At core, FM is a giant interrelated database that just happens to be about football.

The 'just one more go' feeling stems from an innate human desire to impose order onto chaos, whether through banal daily routines, or complex formulas. There's always the feeling you can 'fix' bad decisions, or improve even when things are going well – exacerbated by the game's tight feedback loops.

Aside from the broad objective of winning games, you can set yourself achievable micro-tasks, like building a new backroom team, or scouting a top RB for less than £25k. In short, it's never, ever, boring.

It's known when to evolve, even when little was wrong, like Manchester United's tactical evolution under Carlos Queiroz. FM's scouting network and vast player database is still peerless, while its online communities are vibrant and well served. Every yearly update directly addresses fans' feedback, and bug fixes are regularly applied. Equally, FM has never been afraid to make contentious changes, like the initially disliked in-game match engine – now you can't imagine FM without it. Miles Jacobson is an active evangelist for his brand, and happy to speak to anyone. FM Live was a mixed success, but a bold attempt to harness the power of social networks. Even now, people in work play FM by 'taking turns' on one computer. Rivals can't compete with FM's scale, quality, authenticity and the 'peer pressure' impact of its networked community.

It's even casting an influence outside its genre. Console football games dabble with management modes, and during the mid-2000s, Pro Evolution Soccer's engrossing Master League mode played a key role in its critical superiority over FIFA. Much like FM, Pro Evo's Master League offered a huge, authentic, player database, with player stats that evolved subject to performance. FIFA fought back with an increasingly authentic Manager Mode – in fact, one of FIFA 13's most requested features is richer atmosphere, plus transfer market and tactical depth to rival FM.

Iain Macintosh

THE EMPATHY MACHINE

Iain Macintosh
Co–Author, Football Manager Stole My Life.

IAIN MACINTOSH is co-author of this book and one of Twitter's 'Football 50', the social network's most influential voices on the game, according to TEAMtalk . He believes that his addiction to FM has actually helped his development as a writer. That's what he tells himself anyway.

The Football Manager games have been a constant companion to me for the past 20 years, much as heroin was a constant companion to the cast of Trainspotting. I asked my wife to sum the game up in one line and she just scowled in silent distaste, which I think paints a picture more profound than any words could hope to emulate. And she only met me in 2005. She wasn't around for the darker days. The days when I convinced my parents I was revising for my GCSEs when I was actually guiding a Nii Lamptey-infused West Ham side to the Premier League title. The days at university, when I put so much work in to my Southend United team that I overslept and missed February. The days when I would walk out of my mind-meltingly dull data entry job on a Friday evening, buy a selection of frozen pizzas and tea-bags, and then play through to Sunday night, restoring Aberdeen to the pinnacle of Scottish football.

The present-day reality, an occasional hour-long session while she's watching X-Factor, is like Oliver Reed supping a lemonade shandy to a disapproving glare.

I can honestly say that I wouldn't be here had it not been for these games. I don't mean that in a mortal way – my laptop didn't stop a bullet or anything – I mean here, writing for a living. Like Rory Smith, this game gave me the wealth of knowledge I needed to understand an increasingly global game, but I think its greatest gift to me was empathy. I don't know if I really have a writing style, beyond frantically slapping the keyboard like a chimpanzee and hoping that something half-decent appears, but I have noticed that I tend to be more sympathetic than other journalists. It could be just that I'm too soft-hearted to ever prosper in this industry, but I think the truth is that I'm yet to come across a situation in life that I haven't experienced in the alternative reality of my musky bedroom.

I've taken the mantle of a legend, I've worked my way from the bottom to the top, I've tried in vain to haul a club out of a nose-dive and I've come to realise that real football managers aren't actually know-nothing morons stealing a living. They're experienced football men doing their very best to succeed against the odds. They are my brothers.

Not everyone agrees. Some people think, quite correctly, that the rise of these games has spawned a bastard generation of impatient, unrealistic fools who believe that if they can convince a pile of numbers and variables to over-perform, then it can't be that hard to do it with real people. But you know what? I don't think I'm alone.

I like to think that 20 years of this glorious game, 20 years of bedroom-based toil, has created a legion of like-minded individuals. And I firmly believe that when a hapless manager is twitching in his technical area, suffering the slings and arrows of outrageous fortune, at least one person in the stand behind him is thinking, "Chin up, gaffer. I've been here. And I came through it."

FM at the Euros

MARIO MANDZUKIC

In FM10, the Dinamo Zagreb man was a good team player who thrived in the big matches. How right those eagle-eyed scouts were! Mandzukic was a bargain buy whose value would multiply ten-fold before you'd even had a chance to really get to know each other. Now 26, he joined Bayern Munich after scoring three goals for an impressive Croatia side at Euro 2012.

PAOLO NUTINI SI Towers, 2010

I had an early soundcheck and I think I watched...*sings* I want to know what love iiiisss...Foreigner; we saw Foreigner soundcheck, with their choir. Then in between trying to get a glimpse of Led Zeppelin, I was deep into...I think it was Nottingham Forest at the time, giving myself a challenge. I did OK.

PAOLO NUTINI went in to SI Towers to test drive FM 2010, where Miles Jacobson asked him to clarify a story about how he had spent his time before a huge gig - supporting Led Zeppelin. You can see a lot more of this interview on YouTube...

CHARITY SHIELD

Gaming4Charity
By Rik Molloy

My friends Alex, Jake, Tom and I were playing a network game and talking over Skype. We realised we had 2000 subscribers from the Football Manager community. I suggested that audience should be put to good use.

We decided to raise money for Cancer Research UK, as we've all been affected by cancer in one way or another. We eventually agreed on a 24-hour network game that we would stream live – with a donation page for people to chip in as we went along.

Five days beforehand we received a single donation of £1000, which blew us away and made us rethink our original target of £500. Jake took it to the next level when he managed to get hold of the Reading striker, Adam Le Fondre, who, to our amazement, agreed to join in. The donation page was retweeted by Miles Jacobson at Sports Interactive, which gave us great exposure.

When the big day arrived we were stocked up with coffee, food and a load of Red Bull, while we were inundated with questions for Adam. We had moderators in a chat room posting the donation link every five minutes, while we encouraged the viewers to tweet celebrities to generate some publicity.

Even between the hours of 3-5am we still had hundreds of people watching and talking to us.

Donations poured in from the likes of Bryan Swanson at Sky Sports News and the BBC's Manish Bhasin – as well as Adam and Miles.

In total we received 115 separate donations which raised £2,288.99, so now we're looking to turn it into an annual event for different charities.

Playing for 24 hours isn't easy but we're all crazy on the game, so you can hardly call it a chore. It also shows the power of the Football Manager community, especially when it's complemented by social media. In this case it will hopefully help change lives.

http://www.justgiving.com/gaming4charity

ADAM LE FONDRE
(Reading striker and massive Football Manager fan)

I plugged the fundraiser and took part from around 7pm-2am. By the time I quit I was top of the Premier League with Chelsea. It was a great cause and I was delighted to help.

I play the game religiously. I remember I won the Serie A title with Juventus 10 years in a row but it took me five seasons to win the Champions League. In that first final I had sweaty palms and was just generally nervous. I can't think of any other computer game that would do that to you!

Quite a few of the Reading lads play and I always get tweets from supporters telling me how many goals I've score for their Football Manager team. It's quite surreal but I understand their obsession. I feel the same way.

EXTREME FM

And you thought wearing a suit
for a cup final was a big deal

People are strange, as The Doors once sang, and to prove it, here are some of
the more bizarre things some of you get up to in order to keep it real. Don't try
this at home. Actually, most of these are perfectly safe, knock yourself out

SUIT UP

The starting point. If you don't dress up for the big
occasions, you can't think about this stuff. It's going
to blow your mind. You get through that semi-final,
you know you're going to have to get measured. If
you don't wear a suit for a cup final, it's like you're
just playing a computer game.

XFM tip: Old suit looking a bit tired? Why not
complete the look with a fresh carnation in the
button hole? Won the final? Why not top it off with
a scarf and novelty hat, thrown on to the pitch by an
adoring supporter during your lap of honour.

TOP TUNES

Music. Makes the people. Come together. So sang Madonna and as manager, you want to pack out stadiums just like her, using tactical genius where the ageing pop queen favours fishnet and calisthenics.

- **Champions League** You'll need to download Handel's Zadok the Priest. A search for 'Champions League theme music' will do the job, but know this music existed before Uefa put it on their mixtape.

- **FA Cup final** Tradition dictates you need the hymn Abide With Me. It's okay to cry, but try not to let your players see you. It's confusing for them.

- **International job?** You're going to have to keep on top of national anthems. And remember, Kazakhstan deserves the proper respect. We don't do Borat.

- **Supporters' anthems.** For example, Liverpool and Celtic managers should fire up You'll Never Walk Alone five minutes from full-time. After a home win at the Camp Nou, the Barca hymn should ring out. Find out if your club has an anthem. Make it authentic. Playing Into the Valley by The Skids before every home game may be reason enough to start a new save as manager of Dunfermline Athletic.

GIVE YOURSELF A SHAKE

It only takes a second, but the pre-match manager's handshake is a key scene-setter to the contest ahead. Some of you use the doorknob of the room you play in as the opposing manager's 'hand'. We're not judging.

XFM tip: Remember to factor in your relationship with the manager on a game-by-game basis. Mutual admiration? A good firm grip, plenty of eye (door) contact. Adversarial comments in the press? A cursory tickle while looking out of the window. Out-and-out vendetta? Offer the hand then withdraw, pretending that you were just fixing your hair.

MEET THE FAMILY

At least one of you takes the handshakes to the next level on FA Cup final day, moving down the team line, introducing the attending member of the royal family to your players.

XFM tip: Remember, no kissing.

CLIMATE CHANGE

Away in Europe? A quick check on the seasonal forecast in the country you are visiting should provide you with all you need to up the realism stakes yet further.

A trip to Ukraine on a bitter November night should be undertaken with the window open and your hands in the pockets of your navy blue, knee-length quilted manager's jacket. Away to one of the fanatically-supported Turkish giants? Complete your 'Welcome to Hell' by setting fire to some newspaper for that hard-to-acquire flare/smoke bomb combo effect (thank you, Fudge from the Pie and Bovril forum)

MEET THE PRESS

Your dealings with the press are an essential part of your career and many of you get in as much practice as possible. Lining up teddy bears and/ or action figures post-match may not sound like your thing, but don't knock it until you try it. Just as popular is the in-shower press con, prompting co-habitants to wonder if that's the latest Plan B you're riffing on under the power jet. Not unless his new song's called It Was Never Offside and I Hope They Realise It's Cost Us The Game.

DOING A BUNK

Simple yet brilliantly effective, although exclusive to players in a room with bunk beds. Increase the pain of that touchline ban by sitting on the top bunk during the match.

BUS PASS ——————————————————

Thanks to Tony Jameson, the Newcastle-based comedian preparing a Football Manager show for the 2013 Edinburgh Festival for this one. Winning a trophy for a provincial club can be a once-in-a-lifetime experience for supporters and brings an entire community together. Why deny them the gala atmosphere that surrounds an open-top bus tour? Most large settlements offer open-top tours, especially in the summer, and a small trophy can be purchased at little cost. Raise it aloft to passers-by and watch their chests swell with civic pride.

XFM tip: Try to imagine that the tour guide's commentary is in fact a club official introducing your players to the crowds that have slowed your bus's progress through town to a crawl.

THE PRICE IS RIGHT ——————————————————

This is from the Football Ramble forum, posted by Juan Flo Evra The Cocu's Nesta. Drink that in. And move on.

"My friend told me about a network game with his housemate. It all started when he found a specific player through his scouts. He was arranging a deal, when the other housemate spotted it. He liked the look of that player too and duly bid. The other housemate offered him £20 in real life to stop him from bidding. Since then they've been offering each other incentives and bribes for favourable results, fielding weakened teams, arranging transfer deals etc."

SCOUT'S HONOUR

Football Ramble again. TV Party gives us the only instance we found of real-life scouting for FM players.

"I was playing as Barnet in season 2000/01 and negotiating the signing of Dale Watkins from Cheltenham. Barnet were broke and Cheltenham wanted a bit more than I was willing to pay.

"I decided I needed to sleep on it and the next day went to visit a mate who happened to go to university in Cheltenham. Watching Football Focus, I realised Cheltenham were due to play Bristol Rovers at home. Seeing this as a good opportunity for a scouting trip, I convinced my mate to go to the game and sit through a horrendous bore draw in the worst weather imaginable. Dale Watkins didn't even play. I cancelled the transfer as soon as I got home and never looked back."

THE RETIRING TYPE

The psychological realism possible within FM is almost without bottom. However, our favourite example comes from Andrew Coyle, who started a game as St Mirren in CM 01/02 but was soon poached by Rangers. There, he signed a young striker from Asteras called Alexandros Papadopolous.

The Greek goal machine powered Rangers to four Champions League titles and made Greece European Champions in 2004. As he grew older, he became captain, then player-coach and finally player-assistant manager of Rangers.

"Two conflicting thoughts were in my mind," writes Andrew. "On one hand, winning everything easily was becoming boring. On the other, Papadopolous was well past 900 goals for the club. I decided I would stick with the game until the landmark 1000th Papadopolous goal and then step aside. As a club legend who had also been my coach and assistant, I wanted to see Papapolous appointed as my successor, so I decided to resign, not retire, and watch what developed.

"The historic day came and Papadopolous scored goal number 1000 in the first half. I subbed him as soon as it was scored, just to mark the occasion.

"After the game, I resigned from the club, but only after an emotional and imaginary media conference. I then sat back, waiting to see my protege enjoy his golden moment. Rangers stalled on making the appointment, but I wasn't worried. Who else would they choose?

"Unbelievably, instead of a record-breaking, 1000-goal scoring, multiple European Cup winning player, coach and assistant manager, Rangers appointed former Celtic manager Davie Hay, who hadn't had a job for seven years. I shouted, swore, switched off my PC and didn't touch ChampMan for a year and a half."

FM at the Euros
. I at the Euros

MATS HUMMELS AND HOLGER BADSTUBER

The German centre-back pairing could be in place for a decade and both followed similar career paths if you raided the Bayern Munich reserves for them in FM09. In real life, Hummels, viewed as a defensive midfielder by the Bayern coaches, was loaned and then sold to Borussia Dortmund. It proved a costly decision, as he became the defensive kingpin in back-to-back Bundesliga-winning teams. If only the Bayern coaching staff played FM!

JAMES CORDEN BBC Comic Relief

"I didn't do much except sit around playing Championship Manager – which is without question the finest computer game that's ever been invented. I still play it now from time to time, though it's called Football Manager these days. Let me just take this moment to say thank you to everyone who ever worked on that game. You are all geniuses and I love you all."

In his autobiography, **JAMES CORDEN** reveals the inspiration behind Smithy's famous team talk to the England team for the BBC's Comic Relief.

THE HEIDENHEIM CHRONICLES

by Iain Macintosh

In 2010, light on work and with time to kill, I rattled out my first ever piece of Football Manager fiction. Messy, experimental and deeply narcissistic, I really didn't think that anyone in their right mind would ever be interested and I was absolutely right. What I failed to realise was that there are plenty of people out there in their wrong mind. I expected about 50 hits. I ended up with tens of thousands. The cult success of the story, which ended after 10 episodes, led to work with Official Playstation Magazine, Sports Illustrated and, ultimately, to the longer 'The Ballad of Bobby Manager', published by The Blizzard. That one afternoon of pissing about on Football Manager turned out to be one of the most pivotal moments of my brief and largely inconsequential career as a freelance writer. It's a funny old game.

I have to admit, I thought it was a wind-up at first. I mean, who wouldn't?

"Herr Macintosh," wheezed the voice. "Long have we admired your work."

"I beg your pardon?" I asked, pulling the phone away from my ear to check the number again. 0049. Where was that?

"Long have we admired your work," repeated the voice patiently. "Your columns, your match reports, even that feature where you described Harry Redknapp as a top class manager. How we laughed at that one! You may not realise it, but your Football Fables is now on the required reading list for all Bavarian students and there is much talk of a mini-series based upon your opus Everything You Ever Need To Know About Golf. They're thinking of casting Andreas Brehme as the narrator, you know."

"I'm sorry, who is this?" I laughed, glancing around for Jeremy Beadle and then remembering... mourning...bearing that familiar pang of sadness at his loss.

"My name is Thomas Zacher. I am the chairman of Heidenheim. I have a business proposition for you."

"Heidi Heim?" I burbled. "Is that a fashion label? What do you want with me?"

"We are not a fashion label, Herr Macintosh. We are a football club. A football club that needs your help."

"Ah, right," I said quickly. "I get your drift. Well listen, I don't write for free, not since that thing with 'The Locker Room'. If I'm going to get savaged by the press, I want some decent money first. Or cuddles, you can pay me in cuddles. I can do your player interviews for £50 a throw, columns are double and if I'm ghosting the manager's foreword, I need his notes typed and sent to me 24 hours before deadline."

"You misunderstand, Herr Macintosh. I don't want you to write about the club. I want you to manage the club."

"Manage which bit?"

"The team. I want you to manage my team."

"I'm not with you."

"Be the manager, Herr Macintosh."

"Eh?"

"Sit in the dug-out, pick the team, make the funny hand signals that look like you're trying to push an invisible block of ice across a table. Coach my team. Lead them to glory. Take us from the third flight to the promised land of the Bundesliga. Take our dreams, feather their wings and release them into the sunset. Do you understand?"

"No."

"Look, I'll pay you two thousand of your English pounds a week to be a football manager. Get a taxi, go to the airport, fly to Germany and we'll give you a tracksuit with 'IM' on it."

"You want me to be the manager?"

"Ja."

"I've got one question."

"Ja?"

"Did you *really* like Football Fables?"

PT.2

The ball sailed silently over the back of the stands and away, lost forever in a maze of winding streets.

"Alex?" I called to my only coach. "Can you get another bag of balls, mate?" I glared at Dieter Jarosch, the guilty culprit. Again. "That's four you've lost now, Dieter," I bellowed, holding up my fingers just in case he didn't understand. "Four! Do you think we're made of money? I'm supposed to be building a Bundesliga team here, not overseeing the delivery of a €20 football to every f***ing child in the surrounding area. Keep the f***ing thing down!"

Dieter Jarosch scratched his bottom and stared at the floor. I'd been told that the big 28-year-old had scored goals for fun back in the amateur leagues, but for the life of me I couldn't fathom how. He was like Ian Ormondroyd, but without the former Aston Villa striker's natural grace and poise.

Alex emerged from the tunnel, dragging a sack of balls behind him like a particularly sporty Santa. He hauled one out, gave it a perfunctory squeeze, and then booted it onto the pitch.

"They are doing well!" he grinned as he took his place next to me on the bench.

"Which team?" I asked. Alex had arranged an early practice game between the seniors and the youths and, at that moment, still goalless, it was hard to tell which team was which. I wouldn't mind, but the eldest youth player was 15. They should have been out trying to buy fags and cider, not holding their own against a team of professional footballers. I watched helplessly as Bernd Maier, my captain and a veteran of the regional leagues, tried to play a simple pass to Turkish striker Faruk Gul, missing him by about six yards.

I groaned and began to repeatedly bounce my head off the side of the dug-out.

"Ha! Come on," laughed Alex. "It is not that bad. At least they are trying to pass the ball. They have never done that before. Usually they just try to kick the brand name off of it. You have made them think about their game."

I looked up, just as Marc Schnatterer chased a loose ball off the pitch, slowing down too late to avoid the advertising hoardings.

"They've not exactly got to think about much, Alex," I said as Schnatterer screamed and vanished into the first row of seats with a crash. "It's 4-4-2, I've told them to keep it simple, pass it short, man-to-man mark and just go out and enjoy themselves.

"Exactly," said Alex. "You know, for an English manager, you are very forward-thinking."

"I'm not a manager though," I groaned. "I'm a journalist. I should be up in that press box, eating my own body weight in sausages, stopping only to spell someone's name wrong. I should be unleashing another ill-considered opinion that only popped in to my head while I was on the loo this morning. I should be desperately trying to crowbar references to current affairs into my opening paragraph or covering up my ignorance by basing all my stories on the suggestions of vague 'sources'. That's my football pitch, Alex. That's where I earn my money. I can't do this!"

"Yes, you can!" Alex snapped and he slapped me hard in the face with the back of his hand, as if I were a puppy who had urinated in his slippers. My cheek flushed bright red and the tears came quickly. Alex turned away in disgust.

Back on the pitch, Christian Gmuder slammed a snapshot past youth goalkeeper Uwe Proll, a ginger-headed child who was yet to embark upon his first shave. Bernd Maier roared in delight. I just sat quietly, biting my lip.

"I am sorry," said Alex, staring at the floor. "I will understand if you want to dismiss me."

"I'm not going to dismiss you, Alex," I said as I tried to rub some life back into my cheek. The skin glowed like the light on a strip club door. Alexander Raaf was a powerful bastard, built like a gorilla with hands like snow shovels. Just 35, he'd been with Heidenheim for years, a failure as a player, but an inspiration from the sidelines. He wasn't a tactical genius or a master of technique, he was a motivator and the kids loved him as much as they feared him.

"You should dismiss me," he mumbled. "I should not have struck you."

"No," I shook my head. "You shouldn't. But I needed telling. I just don't know where to start with this lot. They make Southend United look the 1982 Brazilian World Cup squad. They'll pass kidney stones before they pass the ball with any accuracy."

"Can I ask you a question, Iain?" Alex said, turning to face me.

"Of course."

"Did you know where to start when you wrote Football Fables?"

"You've read Football Fables?"

"Of course, I have. Everyone has. It is my son's favourite. He makes me read it to him every night."

"Seriously?"

"Yes," said Alex with a solemn nod. "He particularly likes the double chapter on Brian Clough, where Tony Woodcock and Viv Anderson recount their favourite memories of the man we all knew as 'Old Big 'Ead'. Myself, I would rather read Chopper Harris' chilling recollection of the 1970 FA Cup final, but you know how kids are. Demanding."

"I see."

"But did you know where to start, Iain?"

"No," I admitted. "I don't suppose I did. When you set out to produce an amusing and accessible collection of anecdotes from some of football's most enduring characters, it can be daunting. I felt like Columbus aboard the Santa Maria, heading out across the Atlantic, not knowing whether I would ever see land again."

"Of course you did," smiled Alex. "But you did see land again. You wrote Football Fables, you brought those characters together and you told their stories. You gave my son, and so many people's sons, a priceless gift. And you can do this."

"Can I? Can I really?"

"Yes," smiled Alex. "Of course you can. And I'll be here to help you."

The big German extended his hand. I took it in my own. It felt like chain mail.

"We *can* do it, Alex. We've got three friendlies to kick them into shape and then the season starts. It's a big ask, but if we work together, there's nothing we can't achieve."

There was a dull thump and a collective groan from the pitch.

"DIETER! That's five now, you gormless erection. No more new balls! You can fucking well climb over the stand and get that one back. No I'm not fucking joking! No! No, don't shake your head at me, you lumbering fanny. Get out!"

Alex smiled. "See?" he said. "This is why we wanted an English manager."

PT.3

Das Football Boots – Aired July 20, 2009 – 1830:00 CET

THIS IS A RUSH TRANSCRIPT. THIS COPY MAY NOT BE IN ITS FINAL FORM AND MAY BE UPDATED.

ANCHOR – ...and was eventually apprehended in the ladies lavatory of a restaurant in Gross-Rohrheim. More on the Bundesliga later, but first let's take a trip to the backwaters of the Third Division to catch up with newly-promoted Heidenheim. Lothar Gerber travelled to Bavaria to examine the curious case of an English writer turned German football manager.

VT – *Anonymous looking footballers in white shirts pass the ball to each other in front of a sparse crowd in a small stadium.*

VOICEOVER – 1. Fußballclub Heidenheim 1846. Minnows in a fishtank full of barracuda. Hungry barracuda. You know, the kind of hungry, angry barracuda who, if they were asked to list their favourite food would say 'minnows' without even hesitating or giving a second thought to ice cream or sausages or anything. Heidenheim are crap. But they're here. Here in the Third Division. Without a hope of sticking around, surely?

VT – *A skinny man in a grey suit shakes hands with a wizened old man as a handful of flash bulbs go off in front of them. He leans over a desk and puts pen to paper*

VOICEOVER – Enter Iain Macintosh. You know him as the author of Football Fables, the book that Jurgen Klinsmann once claimed was, "as important as Crime and Punishment.". Well, now he's the manager of Heidenheim. He has no experience, no command of the German language and, if you believe the papers, no chance of keeping his team in the Third Division.

IAIN MACINTOSH (sat in a restaurant, a glass of red wine on table) – Bobbins. We've got every chance of staying up.

> LOTHAR GERBER – *You're a long way from the Stamford Bridge press box though, surely this is going to be quite a challenge?*

IM – Of course it will be a challenge, but I'm ready for it. And I tell you, the Stamford Bridge press box is no walk in the park. It's a bloody minefield. Garth Crooks asked me where the toilet was once. It took him 20 minutes. I nearly missed the last tube.

> LG – *But how can a writer with no coaching credentials hope to succeed as a manager?*

IM – I know football, Lothar, and I know what it takes to win. I've seen a few managers come and go and I doubt that I'm worse than all of them. I mean, come on. Avram Grant? Saw him crap himself at White Hart Lane once, lost a 3-1 lead, was lucky to get out with a 4-4 draw. Started throwing defenders on willy-nilly, it was extraordinary. Anyway, my philosophy is simple. Pass the ball, cherish it. Keep it guarded and don't let anyone else have it. Start from that point and you'll be fine.

> LG – *But what about tactics, set-pieces, that kind of thing?*

IM – Yes.

    LG – Yes what?

IM – Yes, we do them too.

    LG – How do you do them?

Silence

    LG – Iain?

IM – I haven't decided yet.

    LG – Well, what have you been doing in the friendlies?

IM – I ... erm ... Well, I ... erm ... left it to the lads. Keep it simple, know what I mean?

    LG – You forgot, didn't you?

IM – Yes. Yes, I did.

    LG – Let's move on. Transfers. You've signed a lot of players in a short space of time. Why all the reinforcements?

IM – I had to, Lothar. I'll be honest, half the players there are worse than you, and you're a fat lad. I've transfer listed 11 of them, but I can't find anyone daft enough to take them off my hands. Alexander Raaf, my coach, he had a few ideas, so we took a load of lads on trial and tested them out. Christian Lenze, an experienced midfielder from the lower leagues. He can actually pass a ball, so he might not fit in here. Rachid El Hammouchi, he'll give us some pace on the flanks. Clement Halet, the French lad, he's way too good for us, but he'll do until someone good notices that he's batting below his average. Then there's the youngster Zlatan Alomerovic. I can't believe Dortmund let him go.

    LG – Is there anyone you didn't sign after a trial?

IM – Yeah. Tezcan Kerabulet.

    LG – Not good enough?

IM – Oh no, he was a fine player. Just a bit odd.

    LG – How so?

IM – Starts fires.

    LG – I see. So, were you pleased with the friendlies?

IM – Very pleased. We did very well. Very impressive.

    LG – You didn't win any, did you?

IM – No. Not as such.

    LG – Apart from a game behind closed doors. Against a team of 14-year-olds. You won that by a single goal. Late on.

IM – You can only beat what's in front of you, Lothar.

    LG – Iain, can I be frank?

IM – Of course.

    LG – Is this just a publicity stunt?

IM – Absolutely not. This is real. This is my new life now. I promise you that when we take to the field against Unterhaching this weekend, we'll be the best prepared team in all of Germany.

    LG – You're not playing Unterhaching this weekend.

IM – I beg your pardon?

    LG – You're playing Erfut.

IM – Yes, that's what I said.

    LG – No, it wasn't.

IM – Yes it was, check your tape. Erput. That's who we've got.

    LG – *Erfut.*

IM – Yes.

    LG – *Iain, why did Thomas Zacher hire you?*

IM – I have no idea. He just said that he really liked Football Fables.

    LG – *Fair play. It's a fucking great read, that.*

FADEOUT

PT.4

"Iain? Iain, are you in here?" Alex walked along the line of toilet cubicles, slapping his baking tray sized palms against every door until he found the one that was locked. My one. "Iain?"

"I'm not coming out." I whispered. "I don't want to."

"Come on, Iain. The press are becoming restless. You must speak to them. They have eaten all of the biscuits, soon they will anger."

"*You* speak to them."

"I am not going to speak to them. That is not my job. I put cones out. It is a good job."

"You're still angry about Alfred, aren't you?"

"Not at all," Alex said, slightly too quickly. "You needed an assistant manager. There is no reason why you should not have taken one. My feelings are not important."

"I'm not coming out, Alex."

"You must. Things are never as bad as they seem."

"Not as bad as they seem?! We lost 5-0! Erfut took us out on to the pitch, pulled our trousers and pants down and spanked us in front of everyone!"

"We dominated possession," said Alex thoughtfully. "That was one of your aims."

"Yes, but the other aim was not to ship five fucking goals. The first one, what the hell was Tim Gohlert doing? He just stood there scratching his balls. Florian Krebs did the same for the second one. What did we tell them? Fight for everything! They didn't fight for shit!"

"But we enjoyed the better of the second half."

"For 25 minutes!"

"That is the better of the second half."

"Not when they score three goals in the other 20!"

"Calm yourself. The season is long. We have time to regroup. Come out and do the press conference."

I slid the lock across and allowed the door to swing open. Alex peered into the gloom and then swiftly recoiled.

"You have ... erm ... you have vomit on your shirt," he said.

"Yes, I know."

"And your trousers."

"Yes, I know."

"And ... how did you get it in your shoes?"

"I don't know, Alex."

FM at the Euros

ANDREA PIRLO

Italy's player of the tournament was keeping it old school for all the CM01/02 junkies out there. When the vintage edition of the game was released, Pirlo's future was uncertain. He had been at Internazionale for three years, but loaned to Reggina and Brescia. At the time CM01/02 picked him out as an undervalued player at Inter, their great rivals, Milan, reached the same conclusion, paying £15m for the 21-year-old who enjoyed an Indian summer at Euro 2012.

FM at the Euros

ROBERT LEWANDOWSKI

The hero of the home nation and the scorer of the first goal of the competition, Lewndowski was an incredibly early pick by FM's Polish researchers and was on the radar of fans of the game long before Borussia Dortmund made him the focal point of the Bundesliga champions. When FM09 was released Lewandowski had just joined Lech Poznan after top-scoring in the Polish second division with Znicz Pruszków yet was still programmed to achieve great things.

He stepped into the cubicle and hauled me off the seat like a child.

"Come on, Gaffer. That is what they say in England, is it not? Gaffer? Clean yourself."

He dragged me to the sink and turned on the taps. I stooped down and threw cold water over myself before trying to shake the heavier chunks of sick off my collar. They landed on the floor with a series of dull, wet slaps.

"I tried to shake things up," I said, rubbing my eyes. "I went 4-3-3 with the full-backs pushing all the way. I really thought that would work."

"It did work, for a time," said Alex, staring at the floor in horror.

"Then they figured it out. Then they started lumping everything down the wings. If we'd just have taken one of our chances it could all have been so different." I straightened up and looked Alex directly in the eye. "Tell me, is Dieter Jarosh actually a footballer? Is he? Or is he just a bloke who sneaked in one morning and has been here for so long that everyone's got used to him?"

"He used to score many goals," Alex said.

"Well, he's not scoring them now. He's out. And Patrick Mayer too, the blundering tit-bag."

"What are you going to do?" asked Alex.

"I don't know," I said, drying myself down with toilet roll. "But I've got to do something. Where are the players?"

"They went home. They do not like to be shouted at. Andreas Spann actually cried when you called him those names. Tell me, what exactly is a 'thundering turd-burger'?"

"I'm not entirely sure. I guess I lost the plot a bit."

"Lost the plot," said Alex thoughtfully, turning the phrase over in his mind. "Yes. Yes, I think you did. You lost the plot, the narrative and the character development. You were halfway through telling Erol Sabanov that he was a butter-fingered wank-bot sent from the future to royally fuck our lives up the nipsy and then boom! All that sick came out of your nose. I was most surprised."

"You and me both. Where are these journalists?"

Alex pointed to the door.

"Out of the changing room, down the corridor and through the second door on the left. They're waiting for you. Here, take these." He handed me a pack of Garibaldi biscuits. "Sometimes it's the only thing that soothes them."

"Well," I announced looking myself up and down in the mirror. "Let's give them something to write about."

"Be careful, Gaffer," said Alex. "Remember that it is a long season."

"It won't be for me, Alex," I said, reaching for the door. "If I don't start winning games soon, it'll be a very short season indeed."

PT.5

Das Football Boots – Aired July 28, 2009 – 22:00 CET

THIS IS A RUSH TRANSCRIPT. THIS COPY MAY NOT BE IN ITS FINAL FORM AND MAY BE UPDATED.

ANCHOR – ...but he later realised, to his horror, that the cream was supposed to be applied externally. More on that later, but now to Lothar Gerber, who returned to Heidenheim to see hack-turned-gaffer Iain Macintosh in his first home game of the season. Lothar caught up with him in the tunnel, but I bet he now wishes he hadn't...

CUT TO TUNNEL

Lothar Gerber – Iain! Iain Macintosh! Can we have a quick word for 'Das Football Boots'?

> *Iain Macintosh – Lothar! How are you, big man? Still chunky! What did you think, eh? I told you it would happen! (he kisses Lothar on the cheek)*

LG – (squirms) Yes, thank you. Stop it. Stop it! That's better. I'm very pleased for you, but you must have been worried when Aue took the lead?

> *IM – I was, because it was another sloppy goal to give away, but we'd been good up until that point. Really, really good. As good as we've been. Which is good. Isn't it?*

LG – Indeed. There was a new look to the team, explain your thinking?

> *IM – Well, I'd brought in Abdelaziz Ahanfouf on a free and, as you know, he used to play in the top division, so that's a massive signing for us. I couldn't decide who to drop out of Dieter Jarosh and Patrick Mayer, but then I remembered that they're both absolutely*

> *gash, so I binned the pair of them. That allowed me to bring the skipper, Bernd Maier, back in and stick him between the lines to cover those clowns in the defence. He's not quick or, you know, any good at football, but he's experienced, influential and I thought he'd be an example to the others.*

LG – You were obviously right. And he even started the move that led to the equaliser.

> *IM – He did, didn't he? He's clever is Maier. So is Ahanfouf, mind. That little reverse pass he played for Marc Schnatterer was so beautiful that I'd love take it out to the pictures and then try and touch it up in the cab on the way home.*

LG – That's a lovely image.

> *IM – Thank you.*

LG – It was Christian Lenze who set up the next goal to make it 2-1, threading a ball through to that man Schnatterer again. He's another new signing, so that must have pleased you.

> *IM – It did, Lothar. When you take over a team as risible as this one, you've got to bring in bodies quickly. Lenze was head and shoulders above the crap that's been clogging up the shirts here and he showed it with that ball. And another fine finish from Schnatterer as well.*

LG – Aue came back, they scored within minutes to make it 2-2.

IM – *They did, and it was another soft one. A simple ball over the top and their man is clear through. We're going to have to look at that back line. But I don't want to focus on that today, I want to focus on the win. It takes great big balls to put a late penalty away like that and they don't come bigger than Faruk Gul. What nerve he showed there.*

LG – Where does this leave you?

IM – *Mid-table, I'd imagine. Played two, won one, lost one.*

LG – No, I mean, what does it do to expectations?

IM – *We have the same expectations as we always did. We're Heidenheim. We're the worst professional team in Germany. We'll do our best and see what happens.*

LG – Well, if there's any more wheeling and dealing, I'm sure you'll be fine.

IM – *(stiffens) You what?*

LG – (stammering) Erm … I mean, you're quite a wheeler dealer. With all the … erm … players you've …

IM – *(turns to leave) Oh, fuck off.*

LG – What?

IM – *(walking away) Fuck off*

LG – Aw, come on Iain. (pleading) I didn't mean it like that!

IM – *(turns back) Don't call me a fucking wheeler dealer. I'm not a fucking wheeler dealer, I'm a fucking football manager!*

LG – Actually, you're a journalist, aren't you?

IM – *Right, that's it. I'm going to stuff that mic-*

INTERVIEW ENDS

PT.6

I finish my drink. I finish my fag. I get up. I walk to the window. Heidenheim. Heidenheim at night. Much the same as Heidenheim at day. But darker. Darker.

Unterhaching. Dirty dirty Unterhaching. Hateful place. Hateful, spiteful place. Dirty. Dirty, dirty Unterhaching.

I reflect upon another defeat. This time by a single goal. A single, lucky goal. Marcus Steegman. He'll never score another one like that again. Not as long as he lives. Lives. Dies. Dark. Night. One win from three. Underwhelming.

Ralph Hasenhuttl. Manager of Unterhaching. Legend of Austria Vienna. You see him in reception and you stride over to him, hand outstretched, smile on face. But he doesn't see you. He walks straight past you. Ralph heads for his dressing room to give his teamtalk to his players. His special teamtalk with all of his special German words. Unterhaching. Dirty, dirty Unterhaching.

Dieter Jarosh laughed at me today. He didn't think I heard him, but I did. I hear things. He laughed when Marcus Steegman scored. Steegman scored. In. Off. The. Post. Alex leaned over and slapped him upside the head. Faithful Alex. Alexander Raaf. My friend here in Heidenheim. My only friend. My confidante. My partner. But not like that. Straight.

Ralph Hasenhuttl. Staring at you. As if he's never seen a man wearing trainers with a suit before. He's obviously never been to court in Edinburgh. He peers out of his dug-out and examines you. You feel his eyes climbing up you, like ivy up a castle wall. You don't like it. You get scared. You hide behind Alex. Some wee comes out. Dirty trousers. Dirty, dirty trousers.

I pour another drink. I light another fag. It's not fair. Not fair that I sit in this standard Novotel room in the business district of Heidenheim, with its single bed, its strip lighting, its TV without the naughty channels. Not fair that I have to be here alone. I need Ron. I could have done this with Ron. He always had an eye for a player. If I was the front of the shop, he was the front of, well, a much bigger shop. A much, much bigger shop, actually. I pick up the phone.

"Ron?"

"Who the bloody hell is this?" he curses. "Do you know what time it is?"

"Ron, I need you. I can't do this alone. I'm not big enough. But you are."

"Who is this? How did you get this number?"

"They've got it in for me, Ron. Just like Doug Ellis had it in for you. They all have. Dieter. Erol. Clement. Florian. I need you with me. You can make them laugh. You can turn this around. Come on, Ron. It'll be like old times."

"Hang on a minute ... I recognise that voice. Is that you, Iain? I thought I'd got rid of you."

"They hate flair round here, Ron. Hate it and fucking loathe it. Drag it out into the streets and kick it in its guts, kill it and hang it from the lampposts for all to mock and see, from the motorways, from the factories, from the Heidenheim Museum of Clocks."

"Are you drunk? I told you never to phone me again. Don't get me wrong, I liked Football Fables as much as the next man, but the chapter on me feels a little rushed and it focuses too much on things I may or may not have said off-air and not enough on my two FA Cups with Manchester United, or my short-but-exciting period with Atletico Madrid. Now fuck off."

He hangs up. I sit for a moment, cradling the handset to the nape of my neck. Clutching it, as if it were his arm. His great big arm.

Cassio, the Brazilian left-back, is injured. Andreas Spann, the easily-offended midfielder from Ulm, he's injured too. Kicked off the park by dirty, dirty Unterhaching. You've used all your substitutes. Frustration. You want to play yourself, but that would be stupid. You're rubbish. Even worse than Dieter. That's why you took up writing about football. Because you couldn't play it. Couldn't. Shouldn't. Wouldn't. If it was raining. So you sit in your dug-out and you watch. And you lose.

I finish my drink. I finish my fag. I go to the window. The sun peers over the horizon, glum and lethargic like the only remaining headlight of an Austin Allegro. I have no more fags. I have no more drink. I do, however, have a large bottle of Listerine and that might just do the trick. I only want to sleep.

"I don't think much of the biscuits here."

PT.7

Daniel Bolz looked up from his laptop and grunted his agreement at the newcomer before returning to his keyboard, stabbing at the letters with two pointed fingers.

"I said, I don't think much of the biscuits," the stranger repeated, slightly louder this time. "It's not like Sandhausen. We get sausages there. Lots of lovely sausages all sizzling in their own juices. Big fat ones, like Britney's fingers. Mustard too, the whole works."

"I'm working to deadline here," grumbled Daniel without lifting his eyes from the screen.

"Of course, of course. I'll leave you alone."

There was a long pause.

"I'm Klauss, by the way. Klauss Kegl. From the Sandhausen Times."

Daniel sighed in frustration and stopped typing. He stared at his tormentor. A boyish-looking man, probably in his early 30s, Klauss grinned back at him. A single bogey hung from his left nostril like a skinned chicken in the window of a Chinese restaurant.

"You've got something ... something on your nose."

"Have I? Good God, so I have!" He plucked the offending lump from his snout and examined it intently. "My word, look at the size of it. You'd think I'd notice something like that, wouldn't you?" He flicked it hard at the wall, where it stuck like a barnacle to a hull. "Good man!"

"You what?" asked Daniel.

"Good man! It takes a good man to point a booger out to a complete stranger. I could have been walking around all day with that up my nose and I'd have looked a right plonker. Let me buy you a drink."

"There is no drink."

"What? Good Lord, no bar? How's a chap to wet his whistle?"

"There's tea."

"Well, let me get you a tea then!"

"I've already got one."

"Is there anything you would like?"

"I'd like to be able to finish my article."

"Ha ha! Of course, of course."

Klauss sent down in the next chair, disregarding the other seats entirely. Then he stood up again and took off his coat with a flourish that sent drops of rainwater spraying around him, some of them landing on the open laptop.

Daniel grimaced, but stayed silent. This was his first year at the Heidenheim Football Express, his first year out of university, and he wasn't about to end his career prematurely by beating a stranger to death with a second-hand Hewlett-Packard. Far better to rise above it and keep on typing. He'd top-and-tailed his commentary long before half-time. Heidenheim had made his job easier by capitulating long before the end, he just needed to tidy it up before he dropped in whatever cliched nonsense Iain Macintosh was going to unload in this press conference. He stopped typing. Hot breath on his cheek, the smell of old tea and peppermints.

"Do you mind?" he said, without looking up.

"Sorry, sorry!" said Klauss. "I can't help reading over shoulders, it's an awful habit, but I suppose it helps in this line of work, doesn't it?" And he slapped Daniel on the back.

"Haven't you got a deadine?"

"Ha ha! No, no, not at all. We're a weekly, y'see. I won't write this up until tomorrow. Mind you, I'll need all that time just to type out the goalscorers, won't I? Eh? Your mob aren't up to much."

"They're not my mob. I couldn't care less about

them."

"Oh. I see. Well, you must agree that this Macintosh character makes life a little more interesting?"

"I can't stand him."

"How so?"

"He thinks I'm boring. Keeps having a go at me for asking him the same questions all the time. Wanker."

"Oh."

"And it's not like he's even any good, is it?" said Daniel, warming to his theme. "What's he had now? Four games? He lost the first one 0-5, scraped a win, lost to Unterhaching and now this, a 0-4 drubbing at the hands of Sandhausen. He won't last long."

"He's got rather a difficult job on his hands though, hasn't he?"

"He'd make it a lot easier if he could stick to the same tactics. 4-4-2 on the first game, 4-5-1 on the second, then 4-3-3 for the third. And was it today? A lop-sided 4-1-3-1-1?"

"Well, I don't-"

"You think biscuits are the problem here? On the first day of the season he gave us a pack of Garibaldis that tasted of vomit! How does that even happen? And then there was the way he treated poor Lothar. It took the paramedics three hours to get that microphone out. All he did was call him a 'wheeler dealer', and that isn't even offensive, not unless you're desperately trying to cling on to a reputation that never really existed, especially in the face of mounting-"

Klauss gave Daniel a hefty kick under the table.

"Sssh, here he comes."

Iain Macintosh walked into the room and sat down at a small desk towards the front of the room. He glared at Klauss and Daniel.

"Just the two of you?"

They nodded. "Right then," said Iain, folding his arms across his chest. "Let's get started."

"There aren't many positives," began Klauss earnestly.

"No Sherlock, there aren't are there?" interrupted Iain. "That first goal? If I was coaching a team of five-year-olds and they conceded something like that, I'd sneak into their houses on Christmas morning and take a sledgehammer to their presents. And they'd thank me for it. The second one? Like watching a wolf munch his way through a kitten sanctuary. The third? I worry about my defenders. They're the kind of men who drink their own bathwater and lick the windows of the bus. The fourth? Haven't got a clue, wasn't even watching. I was playing Scrabble on the iPhone."

"Iain?" asked Daniel.

"Yes?"

"Stephan Frubeis was pretty solid on his debut. How did you rate his performance?"

"I don't want to comment on individual performances," sighed Iain.

"The public will want to hear a proper answer from you," said Daniel, gulping hard. "Stephan Frubeis was pretty solid on his debut. How did you rate his performance?"

"Stop being a twat, Daniel."

Klauss raised his hand.

"Sherlock?"

"Roberto Pinto had a great game for Sandhuasen," Klauss mumbled.

"Speak up."

"Roberto Pinto had a great game for Sandhausen," he repeated, his voice trembling. "He picked up the man of the match performance. How did you rate his performance?"

"I don't want to comment on individual performances."

There was a long pause. Klauss spoke again.

"The public will want to hear a proper answer from you. Roberto Pinto had a great game for Sandhausen. He picked up the man of the match performance. How did you rate his performance?"

"It's the same thing from you lot every week, isn't it?" said Iain getting to his feet. "Can you not ask me anything original? I wonder why I bother sometimes. I might just start sending my assistant all the time, because there seems little point in even being here. Are you ever going to say something new? Are you?"

"I have a question," said Klauss bravely.

"Go on," said Iain, his eyes flashing with barely concealed contempt.

"Your confidence in your players is admirable. Which do you think is the strongest area of your team? Defence. Midfield. Attack. Or Goalkeeper?"

"Oh, fuck off," spat Iain, and he stormed out.

"See, I told you," said Daniel, after the noise of the slammed door had stopped ringing in his ears "He's a wanker."

PT.8

"I met him in a cell in...erm... somewhere...I was...so down and out.

He...something...me to be the eyes of age ... as he spoke right out.

He talked of life, yes he talked of life. He laughed, clicked heels and he stepped..."

Maggie knew she couldn't really sing that well and she didn't know the words, but she didn't mind. The boys were out in the garden and even if they could hear her off-key falsetto as it drifted out of the open windows, she knew they wouldn't do anything more than give her a gentle ribbing. She didn't mind that either. Banter made the world go round, that's what Ron always said. But where was he this time?

"Mister Bojangles, Mister Bojangles, Mister Bojangles, Dance!"

She continued to buff away at the 1991 Worthington Cup replica they kept on the mantelpiece. Ron used to joke that if he couldn't comb his hair over in its reflection, then it just wasn't shiny enough. And then he'd pinch her bottom. Oh, he could make her feel as giddy as a schoolgirl some mornings.

She heard the key in the door and breathed a sigh of relief. There he was!

"Good morning, my sweetness and light!" he called from the hallway.

"Ron!" she answered back, trying to be stern but missing the mark by miles. "Where have you been? I wasn't in the wide-awake club this morning, so I didn't even hear you leave."

"It wouldn't have mattered if you were in the wide-awake club or not, my princess," said Ron, striding into the living room like a general. "I'd have only given you the eyebrows and slipped out, left lollypop."

"I'll earn that spotter's badge one day," Maggie giggled. "You see if I don't! Now, where have you been?"

"I nipped out to the newsagent early doors, but I found Ken in an awful state."

"What's wrong with him? Have the paperboys been bullying him again?"

"There's your spotter's badge, you sweet, sweet cherry! That's exactly what they've been doing. They've been showing up late, pilfering fags while he's on the bog. One of 'em has even been posting bongo mags through old ladies' doors. Horror show. No team spirit."

"What did you do?"

"The only thing I could, my reason-to-live. I called 'em all into the backroom and put a reducer on the biggest one, just to let him know who the gaffer was. I slapped the second-biggest one for laughing and then I laid the law down. Big Ron's big speech. Then, when I was finished and they were still snivelling about Child Line, I called a minicab and sent them all, Ken included, out for a golf day. Get some smiles on some faces. Ken'll be just fine now."

"Oh, you are clever, love."

"It's what I do. Are the lads here?"

"They certainly are, they're out in the back garden."

"How are they doing? How's Carlton coping with the guttering?"

Maggie pursed her lips. "Well, he's a bit awkward, isn't he? He had some problems with the ladder at first, fell off it twice, but he's really putting a shift in. I couldn't ask any more of the lad. He's not got much in his locker, skill-wise, but he's not short of heart, my angel. I took him a Vimto about 20 minutes ago. He seemed well pleased."

"And Dalian? How's he doing with that lawn?"

"Not as good, love. He started well, a beguiling combination of pace and power that made me think he could achieve anything he wanted to in that garden, but to be honest, it's all gone to pot now. Just take a look out the window."

Ron peered through the net curtains. "What's he doing?"

"I think he's making daisy chains, bless him."

"Alright, I'll have a word."

"Just before you do, love ... we got another one of those messages."

"Oh, Christ. How bad?"

"It's not a good one. It came while I was taking a cup of tea for Deano, he's here fixing up the tree-house. He's not .... he's not right, Ron."

"Deano?"

"No, love. Deano's never been right. I meant this Iain bloke. He's not well."

"Let's have a listen, shall we?"

Maggie shuddered. "Do you mind if I don't, love? It gives me the collywobbles."

Ron nodded and walked out into the hallway. The red light on the answer-machine blinked accusingly. He took a deep breath and pressed the button.

"You have ... one message. Message received on August. The Twenty-Second. To return the call ... press hash."

"Come on," groaned Ron impatiently.

"Are you there, Ron? It's me. Iain. I don't know what I'm doing wrong, Ron. I've improved the squad, I've laid down the law, I've even put the reducer on Dieter Jarolsh. It's not happening. Offenbach. 0-1. We've lost three on the bounce now and I can't see where the next goal is coming from, let alone the next win. What is it, Ron? What's the secret? How did you do it with West Brom? How did you build that confidence ... I tried it with Faruk Gul. I gave him a cuddle. In front of everyone, I gave him a cuddle and told him that he was a world-beater. Now he just thinks I'm a bit weird and the lads all cover themselves when I walk into the dressing room. I took Florian Krebs out for a drink, but I got a bit squiffy and did some sick on his shoes. I went karting with Martin Klarer, but I ran him into the tyre wall and he's out for six weeks with an ankle injury. I can't seem to do anything right. I give biscuits to the press, I treat the staff with respect, but I never get anything back. Apart from Alex. He's great and I probably shouldn't have appointed Alfred over his head in retrospect, especially as he doesn't really help much but ... Oh, Ron, what do I do? What do I ... what... wh..."

"It goes quiet here for a while and then he just cries for five minutes," said Maggie, appearing behind Ron and putting a hand on his shoulder. "Like I said, he's not well."

"We've all felt that pain, Margaret." said Ron with a strange, distant look in his eyes. "We've all felt that loneliness."

Maggie slipped back into the kitchen. He hadn't

called her by her actual name for a long time. A long, long time.

"To delete this message. Press. Three."

Ron reached out and pushed the number three.

"Margaret?" he called out.

"Yes, love?"

"Ask Deano if he's got any plans for the next week, will you?"

"Of course, love."

"And tell Carlton to fire up the Ron-mobile."

"Yes, love."

"And Margaret?"

"Yes, love?"

"Actually, never mind. Probably best just to leave Dalian to his daisy chains, eh?"

PT.9

I opened the door of the boot room and walked headfirst into a wave of sweat and laughter, raw jubilation crashing through the air. I grinned, I closed my eyes and I just let it wash over me like a hot shower after a long, long run.

When I opened my eyes again, Ron was right up in my face, roaring at me.

"I told you! Didn't I tell you? I TOLD YOU! I told you that you could do it! What did I tell him, Carlton?"

"You told him, gaffer," smiled Carlton and he stuck

out one of his enormous arms and ruffled the back of my head.

"Do you want some bubbles, Macca?" squealed Dean Saunders in delight. He thrust a cold bottle of champagne into my hand, excitedly bouncing up and down on the spot like a naughty monkey preparing to throw his poo.

"Easy now, Deano," said Ron. "Let the poor lad get his breath back. Let him take a seat. It's not every day you beat the league leaders." He pulled us both down on to the physio's bench and put his arm round my shoulders. His great big arm.

"But I want him to have it nooooooow!" wailed Deano, stamping his feet and spinning like a dervish.

"Come on then, Deano," I announced, giving Ron a quick grin. "Give us a go on those bubbles."

"Wheeeee!" Deano screamed, which was odd. "You're gonna love it! You're gonna love it!"

I pressed the cold neck of the bottle to my lips, a relief in this tiny room, dense and dank with the fug of man-sweat. I threw my head back. The champagne flowed into my aching, shouted-out throat and burned like acid, its over-powering aftertaste rising up through my nostrils like the bell on a Test Your Strength machine.

"Christ, Deano. That's rancid!" I howled, swallowing hard, desperately hoping that the taste would disappear as quickly as it had arrived.

"Do you wanna know why?" giggled Deano, his eyes so wide that they could have fallen out of his head at any moment. Beside me, Ron's head dropped and I heard Carlton sigh.

"Is it from Portugal?"

"No!" laughed Deano like a horse. "It's 'cos I pissed in it! I pissed in it!"

"For fuck's sake, Deano," groaned Carlton. "Why are you always pissing in the champagne? It was funny the first time, but it's getting really old now."

Deano sank to his knees in hysterics, beating the tiled floor with his fists.

"I'm sorry, Macca, I really am," said Ron. "He's a fucking animal."

"I don't care," I laughed. "I don't care that I've just drunk Dean Saunders' piss. Those three points are more than enough to take the taste away. I never would have believed that we'd beat Eintract Braunschweig, not ever. I mean, they've got Carsten Jancker!"

"That's your problem, son," said Ron. "You don't believe. Take Carlton here. He didn't believe that he could play for England. But he could. I always knew he could. Only 10 per cent of success is out there on the pitch. The other 90 per cent, that's between your ears. If you're mentally strong...."

"You'll not go far wrong," echoed Carlton.

"Exactly," said Ron. "Now pass me the ice bucket. I put one of my good magnums in there and it's still sealed. There's no chance Deano could have got to it."

"Thanks, Ron," I said. I picked up the ice-bucket and handed it to him. "You were right about Florian Krebs. Getting him to man-to-man mark Jancker was a master-stroke."

Ron opened the champagne with a resounding pop, plonked it back in the ice bucket and handed it back to me.

"That's just experience. There's always an angle, always a way to make the difference. In the League Cup final of 1994, we put Deano up front on his own, relying on his intelligence to carve out chances."

We looked down at Deano. He'd gone foetal with the giggles, squirming on the floor, tears streaming down his face, a damp patch spreading steadily across the lap of his tracksuit.

"It was a long time ago," said Ron quickly. "Try the champagne."

The door opened and Alex poked his head round.

"Alex!" I shouted. "We've just opened a bottle! Come and join us!"

"We?" said Alex with a strange look on his face. "Us?"

I looked around. The room was empty. Dirty boots lined the walls, stud-clumps of dirt lay on the floor. It was cold and there was the smell of damp.

"I..." I said. "No-one. No-one. Just me."

Alex stared at me. "Why are you holding the mop bucket?"

I looked down. A filthy mop bucket full of ice looked back at me. In the middle, a jumbo-sized bottle of Listerine bobbed between the cubes. The seal was broken. It was only half-full. An eternity passed by in my mind like a dust-storm.

"Iain?" said Alex.

"I was going to clean the boot-room, Alex. It helps me think."

"Ok, fair enough. I thought I heard voices?"

"Just me," I said. "I like to vocalise my thoughts after a win."

"A win!" laughed Alex. "It's been a while since that happened!"

"What?"

"We lost, gaffer. 0-2. Eintract Braunschweig. Jancker got them both. Are you sure you're alright?"

I looked around the cold, empty boot-room, missing the warmth and the camaraderie and Ron and Carlton, not so much Deano, and the feeling that I'd done something. That I'd achieved. That I was worth it. I missed that feeling like a child misses his mother on the first day of school.

"No, Alex." I said quietly. "I'm not entirely sure that I am."

PT.10

Das Football Boots – Aired July 28, 2009 – 22:00 CET

THIS IS A RUSH TRANSCRIPT. THIS COPY MAY NOT BE IN ITS FINAL FORM AND MAY BE UPDATED.

ANCHOR –...but the squirrels did not consent, announced the judge, and for that reason, a custodial sentence was necessary. More from the Bundesliga later, but now to the backwaters of German football and the strange story of a journalist who waded way out of his depth. It's five years since the mysterious disappearance of Heidenheim manager Iain Macintosh. The Englishman, who arrived at the struggling German club amidst a blaze of publicity, lost nine of his 10 games in charge of the team before walking out of the training ground, never to return. Lothar Gerber speaks to the men who knew him best.

Alex Raaf (Heidenheim 2002 – 2010)
I'll never forget that morning, for sure. None of us will.

Dieter Jarosch (Heidenheim 2007 – Present)
We knew that something was wrong. He couldn't walk through a door until he'd slapped himself in the testicles 14 times. That's not the sign of a healthy mind.

Florian Krebs (Heidenheim 2009 – 2010)
He was sick in the dressing room. Out of his nostrils. While giving a team-talk! Even Joe Kinnear has never done that before.

VT – Footage of Iain Macintosh in a suit, signing terms with the club. Smiling.

Iain Macintosh (2009) – Of course it will be a challenge! But I'm ready for it!

Lothar Gerber (sat on the bench at a deserted Albstadion) – Millions of us play Football Manager every day. On our computers. On our phones. On our specta-consoles. The fantasy of taking control of our favourite football team is over-powering. We all like to think that we know best. We all wish for a chance to find out for real.

(Looks hard at the camera)

Sometimes, you should be careful what you wish for.

Alex Raaf (Heidenheim 2002 – 2010)
Yeah, it was a surprise to us. We knew that the old man was bringing in a manager from left-field, but we didn't ever think it would be that left-field. He wasn't a player, he wasn't a coach. He was a writer. And granted, Football Fables – the true stories of triumph and despair from football's mavericks – was a great book. I'm just not sure that it was enough to prepare him for the rigours of football management.

Dieter Jarosch (Heidenheim 2007 – Present)
Oh God, he was weird from the start. He called me a 'gormless erection' and a 'lumbering fanny' in the same sentence. I mean, can't you see how weird that is? That's a man-part and a lady-part. How can I be both? Crackers. Absolutely crackers. I loathed him.

Florian Krebs (Heidenheim 2009 – 2010)
He tried his best, I guess. He once took me out for a drink to explain the concept of a clearance. First he tried to do it with words, but that didn't help. Then he tried diagrams, but I was still none the wiser. He went down the road, bought a guitar and tried to teach me through the medium of music, but still nothing. I just couldn't see why I shouldn't fanny about in possession on the edge of my own penalty area, oblivious to the threat of oncoming strikers. I mean, what could possibly go wrong? Week in. Week out. Anyway, we were there so long that we both got completely ratted and he chucked up all over my winkle-pickers. Poor man.

VT – Footage of Iain Macintosh rocking backwards and forwards in the dug-out. Subtitles appear. He tells Alex Raaf to sit down. Raaf obeys. Macintosh seems calm. Then he erupts. "What are you sitting down for?" he bellows. "Get up!" And he pushes Raaf off the bench.

Lothar Gerber (sat on the bench at a deserted Albstadion) – The pressure began to tell. Heidenheim were thrashed 0-5 by Erfut. Then they beat Aue 3-2 in a dramatic afternoon in Bavaria. But Macintosh never won another point. Defeats followed with crippling inevitability. Unterhaching (0-1), Sandhausen (0-4), Offenbach (0-1), Eintract Braunschweig (0-2), Dresden (0-2), Jena (1-3), Wuppertal (0-3) and finally, on the 19th of September, to Bayern Munich II (0-6).

Alex Raaf (Heidenheim 2002 – 2010)

I walked into the dressing room the morning after and the smell was unbearable. There were empty bottles of Listerine all over the floor and the words, "WHY HAST THOU FORSAKEN ME, RON?" were scrawled on the walls in excrement. I mean, I'd seen him vomit, I'd seen him cry, I'd seen him talk to a mop bucket and I'd seen him naked. In Starbucks. At 4pm. I have to be honest, though. That was the first time I thought he might be a bit mental.

Dieter Jarosch (Heidenheim 2007 – Present)

It was all so pointless. We were relegated at the end of the season anyway. I don't think anyone could have kept us up. The important thing, and I think the thing that Macintosh always missed, was that we were a team. We share our success and we share our failure. I mean, look at me. I'm 33 and I'm still part of Heidenheim. Obviously I'm semi-professional again now. What do I do as a proper job? Oh, I work in a dairy. It's my job to massage the milk out of the cows by swinging a flat-bottomed instrument against their rear-end. I prefer to use a banjo, personally. Mind you, I'm not very good. I always seem to miss.

Florian Krebs (Heidenheim 2009 – 2010)

I'll miss him. Underneath that snivelling, swearing, sick-splattered wreck of a man, with his lack of understanding of defensive practice, his unabashed amateurism, his violent tantrums and his cruel barbed-...I'm sorry, I've forgotten my original point.

Lothar Gerber (sat on the bench at a deserted Albstadion) – Macintosh left few clues behind. His hotel room was immaculate, save for a discarded copy of 'Championship Manager 2001/02. On the front of the box was the message.

"I was good at this one. Honest. Once I took Southend United into the UEFA Cup."

Some say that he vanished to Asia, others think he now resides in a hippy commune in India. One internet site boasts pictures of him playing with an astronaut, a dinosaur and a potato-headed man, though on closer inspection, that's probably a still of Woody from Toy Story. Perhaps the mystery will never be solved. Perhaps we have seen the last of this ill-mannered English fop and his volcanic temper tantrums. Speaking as someone who once had to have his own microphone surgically removed from his anus, I say 'good riddance'.

Back to you in the studio, Rutger.

ENDS

HIT THE NET

There are many, many places online where you can watch, read or talk FM. Those below have all been helpful in the production of this book and we recommend them to you.

SPORTS INTERACTIVE
http://community.sigames.com/

The home of the friendly and diverse FM community, who were so helpful in producing this book.

FOOTBALL MANAGER:
MORE THAN JUST A GAME
http://www.youtube.com/watch?v=gm-w4EsgLhY

This is one of several FM documentaries on YouTube but we were impressed enough to ask the film maker, Stephen Milnes, to help us out with this book.

CRAP MANAGER
www.crapmanager.info

The home of a fundamentalist sect exiled from the Sports Interactive board who play the game the hard way. Very nice people.

FM SCOUT
www.fmscout.com/

There are many alternative sources of information, opinion and downloads. We like this one a great deal.

THANK YOU!

Football Manager Stole My Life is the result of an almighty team effort. Like any successful club, our squad was methodically assembled with specialists in each position.

Each and every one of the players in 'There's Only One Tonton Zola Moukoko' deserve a 20 for Bravery, for being gracious enough to get involved and, in some cases, have a laugh at their own expense.

Special thanks go to African football expert Gary Al Smith (@garyalsmith) for ensnaring the lesser-spotted Nii Lamptey, and to Rob Middleton (assistant news editor at Northamptonshire Newspapers) for talking us through Justin Georcelin's troubled, short-lived career. Sports journalist Vegard Fl. Vaagbo (@RBFlemma) was our Norwegian knight in shining armour – hooking us up with Tommy Svindal Larsen when all hope looked lost – while Champ Man addicts Omar Smarason of the Icelandic FA and West Brom's Chris Hall, amongst others, bent over backwards to offer their assistance.

We're also grateful to the head researchers – the hustle behind the SI muscle – for offering an insight into the cloak-and-dagger world of scouting.

The response we got from fans of the game when we asked for your stories was extraordinary. It is greatly appreciated, even if your story didn't appear in these pages.

Sports Interactive were generous and supportive without good reason. Particular thanks go to Paul and Ov Collyer, Ciaran Brennan, Alex Bell and Stuart Warren. We took up more of the incredible Miles Jacobson's time than we should have, yet he never said so. And the closer we got to his and SI's staggering work for charities, the more impressive it became.

Iain Macintosh would like to thank his beautiful wife Rachael for putting up with him and for eventually accepting that three weeks of Championship Manager 2001/02 was actually a very necessary part of intensive research. He'd also like to thank his daughter Matilda for being awesome.

Kenny Millar would like to thank his Mum, Lorna for never once begrudging or interrupting a crucial Championship Manager session during those idyllic childhood days in Campbeltown, John Martin for introducing him to 'The Game' in the first place and Jeni, just for being Jeni.

THE WRITERS

IAIN MACINTOSH is a freelance football writer for publications and websites in every corner of the known universe. He is also one of TEAMtalk's Football 50, their list of the top voices on the game to be found on Twitter - judge for yourself @iainmacintosh

KENNY MILLAR is on there too @kenny_millar and by day he is a sports writer with The Sunday Post in Scotland. He is also a veteran of the Battle of Townhead, a brutal weekly five-a-side game between Glasgow's football writers and the closest contemporary Scotland comes to modern warfare

NEIL WHITE is one of three sports journalists who formed BackPage Press in 2009. This is the third BackPage title and they have many more planned. Don't miss a trick by following @backpagepress or finding them on Facebook